ON THE
FUTURE
OF FOOD

REBEL TAKES

ON THE
FUTURE
OF FOOD

CATHERINE JOY WHITE

dialogue
books

DIALOGUE BOOKS

First published in Great Britain in 2024 by Dialogue Books

1 3 5 7 9 10 8 6 4 2

A CIP catalogue record for this book
is available from the British Library.

Paperback ISBN 978-0-349-70263-6

Typeset in Berling by M Rules
Printed and bound in Great Britain by
Clays Ltd, Elcograf S.p.A

Papers used by Dialogue Books are from well-managed forests
and other responsible sources.

Dialogue Books
An imprint of Dialogue
Carmelite House
50 Victoria Embankment
London EC4Y 0DZ

www.dialoguebooks.co.uk

Dialogue, part of Little, Brown Book Group Limited,
an Hachette UK company.

when life gave us lemons
we rose up
started cooking
and changed the world

CONTENTS

PREFACE

A REBELLIOUS TAKE

On the Future of Food is a reimagining of food and a radical visioning of an alternative future. Often overlooked, food and food practices are seen as traditional, archaic, irrelevant and mundane. While we might pay some attention to what it is that we're eating, the majority of us don't overthink the wider social and political implications of food. We eat, we enjoy, we survive – and we move on. Despite this, the possibilities of food are endless. It can shape the way we view the world, transform the way we look, the way we feel and the way we think. It can act as a vehicle for social change, fuelling us as we grow, and yet it can also serve as a symbol of the greatest inequalities: chaining us to a set of circumstances that the world sees no cause for us to rise out of. Gender is one arena where this comes into play with great force. For centuries, the role of domestic chef has twisted itself into the shape of a woman, meaning that food has often been dismissed as a way of upholding patriarchal structures, imprisoning women against their will in an unpaid, unskilled (but essential) labour. And yet, food is also a blueprint to life. It has a rich history and an ever-changing present leading to a future of unknown and expansive potential. It is at every celebration, every union of love, every arrival of life. It accompanies our darkest moments, our last goodbyes. It is an artistic endeavour, an expression of the self – and it is also a means of survival. Food is waking up each morning and getting through; saying yes to another day. It is also, I think, a way of understanding ourselves and understanding each other. It is an insight into other worlds. It is a window – just slightly ajar – and if we look closely enough, we might land upon a legacy, tenderly left for us by generations of cultivators, harvesters, parents, carers, community leaders and nurturers. It is a means of sitting with that legacy, feasting on it and finding new ways of listening to voices that we have so far paid little credence to. Food, for me, is connection. It is a uniting element in the ongoing crafting of our stories and, if I choose to take hold of the possibilities of its narrative, I can see how it is rooted in the sanctuary of our mothers' kitchens.

Part memoir, part recipe, part social commentary, part poetry and part manifesto, On the Future of Food takes us from rural English villages to the pulsing energy of New York City. It takes us from the Khoisan, Southern Africa's Indigenous human habitants, to the environmental activists working to encourage us all to rebuild our relationship with the land. It explores women-led responses to global food security issues alongside women sustaining their communities – crafting entire worlds – from their kitchens. From the women who have been uplifting their families through cooking to the pioneers working to end hunger and those fighting to save our planet, it pays tribute to those who have not typically been heralded. It radically reconsiders the Black and Indigenous cultures foraging for food, tapping into ancestral knowledge but also creating new narratives around sometimes capitalist-commodified concepts such as 'rewilding' that have always existed within Indigenous communities. It will celebrate some of the activists who changed the global food map, meeting trailblazers such as Fannie Lou Hamer and Georgia Gilmore, and those such as Alexis Nicole Nelson who are picking up their mantle today. Sitting right at the heart of this global recipe of radical reimagining are believers who see possibility and are using food to create, to resist, to uplift and, above all else, to bring joy.

The way that food sits in modern culture means that this is becoming urgent. These are topics that we cannot ignore any longer. *On the Future of Food* explores how our overconsumption of meat not only raises a serious moral dilemma, but also directly contributes to the degradation of our planet and our overwhelming environmental footprint. The amount of food that is wasted – simply thrown away by those who don't feel a financial pinch – while we are living in a time of crisis where people are starving to death is astounding. It also explores what I see as the confusing nature of our relationship to food. Discourse has become so clouded that it is hard to know how to feel about it, and even more so how to speak about it. We are living in an era of self-love and body positivity, yet statistics surrounding disordered eating show that it is just as prevalent as ever.

Weight loss drug Ozempic is so popular that diabetics with a genuine medical need are unable to access it. Playing out against the noise of this conflicted discourse are the groups that the statistics leave out; those who aren't seen to be susceptible to the stultifying clutches of wanting to starve yourself until you disappear. We are saturated, bombarded even with this dialogue around food and yet much of it is negative. We need, more than ever, to actively look at how we can turn it around and instead radically use food as a force for good. After all, it is one of the very few things that unites every single person on this planet. As a first step in this, we need to grapple with some of the thorny dilemmas encroaching on our modern society – and propose a new narrative.

On the Future of Food, the first book in the *Rebel Takes* series – a collection of books that dares to dream of an alternative future – faces this head on by fusing the history of food and a vision for its future with possibility. What if we look beyond the expected? This book urges each one of us to really live and breathe the scent of this possibility; to devour it. If we look closely enough, we will see that there are many alternative visions of the narrative that we have grown used to hearing, where the relationship between women and food is solely one of oppression and toil, or where we must eat meat to survive simply because we have always done so. Instead, cooking and food can become an art / a ritual / a sacred act. Food can become a uniting element in our stories; a means of identity creation, economic empowerment, political consciousness raising – and a way of crafting *new* stories. Through exploring food in this way, the door opens for each of us to also consider – or reconsider – our own relationship with food, our heritage and ourselves, seasoned with the promise of a more equitable landscape. Brighter days are coming. I can taste them.

PART I

BIRTH

Starter
noun.

Dish served before a main course.

Where we create, curate and find our feet.

MY MOTHER'S KITCHEN

In my mother's kitchen she is
radical
artist
fearless
creator
sacred
radically imagining
re
imagining
seasoning with the subtle scent of
hope.
In my mother's kitchen you can't hide
from eyes that have already seen it all.
In my mother's kitchen age-old conflicts are laid to rest.
Sermons waft their way
into the ears of the lost
the broken
the burnt out wrought out turned out inside out
but tenderly.
A sweet song
like honey

like syrup
like a marching beat that will not be stopped
but will be sautéed seasoned stirred
With empathy with courage with solidarity with
resilience
In my mother's kitchen community comes first
We cook for ourselves but also for each other
For the hungry
For the weary
For the frozen
also for the triumphant for the dreamers for
the movers and the makers and shakers
In my mother's kitchen we clank plates and
knives and forks and talks as we
share
our days and hopes and fears and dreams
In my mother's kitchen she adds a dash
of honesty to every dish
We try to stomach it
Dancing to sweeten
Knowing that we will swallow because the
dash of honesty is seasoned with love
warm
As ripe plantain
as succulent pineapple
Sharp as lemon
or the most fiery of spices.
Radical love
Ours for the taking
And in our mothers' kitchens the revolution begins.

A DECLARATION OF HOPE

Lemonade out of lemons. Something out of nothing. Yesterday's leftovers reimagined as today's gourmet feast. In the kitchen you can find the creators. The grafters. The crafters. Look hard enough and you will find the weavers of magic. The alchemists who feed families and sustain communities: often behind the scenes, uncredited; often without support or thanks, just expectations. When considering food, we tend to think simply of the final stage: the plates ending up on the tables, the food being consumed before being forgotten about. Yet, trailing back through time – through recipes and cookbooks and creations – we can find stories at every stage of the cooking process, lessons to be devoured from the heart of the foundations. Right from the start. Gathering. Reaping the harvest. Squeezing life from the chicken; a flick of the wrist – a snap of the neck – an ending of life to breathe life into their own. It is the heavy work; the cooking, the baking, the preparing. But it is also the skilful delicacy. The finesse. The cultivating of elegant ingredients, combining of flavours. The kitchen is a hub. It is a movement, and the women at its heart are architects. Designers. Visionaries. We would be wise not to overlook them.

I am a possibilities kind of person. Tell me I can't and I will show you a way. Write something off and I will go back for a final look, just to make sure. If I do nothing else I will search for hope where it seemingly does not exist. I do not believe that we can wait until we have figured out the answers before we decide to pull happiness from the depths of our circumstances. It is a choice. What does the alternative look like? What if we wait so long for the circumstances to be right for us to feel joy that we simply never find it? We must choose to craft it ourselves. That is our declaration of hope. That is our act of becoming. It is our commitment to a belief that things can be different from the way that they have always been.

Food exists in this space of possibility. In fact, it is our way of actioning this declaration. It is a universal daily routine that moves beyond the mundane – requiring thought, creativity, heart, soul and science – while also quite literally keeping us alive. Food is an act of survival. If we don't eat, we won't live. Those who are in the kitchens are survivors, fighters and warriors. They paved the way for us, the consumers, to fully experience food at its most potent: as a means of sustaining communities, collectively building shared histories and actively continuing to resist narratives that would prohibit this. It is more than that though. Yes, food is resistance, but resistance often evokes the thought of a particular form of protest; of staying strong and refusing to shift, no matter what. In our mothers' kitchens, with our declaration of the power of possibility ringing out, food is more than just resistance as immovability. It is resistance as an act of kindness, resistance as softness – soft life – embracing ease and rejecting struggle, resistance as a – temporary – transcendence of the world and its woes.

Food and the way we consume, create and interpret it can be political. I speak to family, strangers, friends. What is it you like about cooking? Why do you dislike it? For everyone who commented on the rhythmic, repetitive nature of cooking as being what they are drawn to, I reflect that what I love is its freedom. American culinary anthropologist Vertamae Smart-Grosvenor recognised this too, writing in her landmark book, *Vibration Cooking: Or, The Travel Notes of a Geechee Girl*: 'And when I cook, I never measure or weigh anything. I cook by vibration. I can tell by the look and smell of it.' Cooking by vibration is not sloppy cooking, but formal expressive practice drawing on deep cultural knowledge: 'If you have any trouble, I suggest you check out your kitchen vibrations. What kind of pots are you using? Throw out all of them except the black ones.'[1]

For Smart-Grosvenor, the process of cooking also starts from a place of optimism and freedom. It is a space where energy, feeling and instinct combine with explosive results. This feels like a kind of cooking that I want to immerse myself in. I start to make my way through cookery books, searching for recipes and anecdotes – blueprints to creating that are not confined by rigid parameters. I am searching for the expansive. I read, reflect and cook, vowing to keep my declaration of joy on my lips as I pursue a radical reimagining that takes me forward; back to move beyond.

I take great inspiration from Smart-Grosvenor, looking courageously forward, single-minded and fearless in my mission as I question how we, through food, can see ourselves as creators. How can we continue cultivating and growing? How can we keep alive the legacy of those who have shaped their lives – and the lives of others – with food? Like many of the women whose lives, complexities and works I lose myself in, Smart-Grosvenor's recipes move beyond simply citing instructions. They are steeped in cultural legacy, fusing food with the generational nuances of creativity and works that have imbued rich histories with a depth that has so often escaped acknowledgement. I toy with the notion that food is just as important as any other type of activism, then dismiss it, feeling foolish. Then, stirring food as an art form into a pot with food as a political act and baking it with food as a means of survival, I reconsider.

Like Smart-Grosvenor before me, I don't measure and weigh. I am not a scientist. I am a human for whom food was once a chain, but now it is an anchor. It is a means of survival. Quite unlike almost all other creative pursuits, its results are nearly immediate. If I throw ingredients together with joy and verve, I will create something. It might not be the most accomplished or the most delicious, but it will be mine: my style, my voice, my taste. Cooking is an art. It is a ritual. It welcomes any one of us, anyone who needs it, even if not all have access to it.

Celebrating those who are no longer with us

We come to the table, we break bread, we pray, we share, we open.

It is an everyday magic.

As I reflect on my own relationship with food, I recognise that sometimes the very practice of consuming food requires a grappling with hard truths about ourselves – or about the world around us. In these instances, food can often be a point of radicalisation, frequently leading to *transformation*.

I first experienced this aged seven in what can only be described, bizarrely, as the most innocent of childhood memories. I watched the animated film *Chicken Run*, initially revelling in the sheer thrill of the chickens' quest for freedom. I willed them to survive and lost myself in their noble endeavour. Then, at some point while watching, a horrifying thought began to form: *what if this isn't just make-believe?* I slowly began to make the connection between the adorable, intelligent and charismatic chickens on the screen in front of me and the lifeless pieces of flesh that I had quite happily eaten without question for the seven years of my life thus far. When the film was over, I asked tearful and probing questions of my parents; a miniature detective determined not to rest until she had her answers. There was very little that my parents could say to reassure me. 'It's just a film' wasn't entirely true, and all three of us knew it. It began to make sense to me. I didn't want the chickens – or any living creature – to die, but I lacked the capacity (at that stage) to personally save them. I couldn't take on every single Mrs Tweedy (the evil mastermind behind *Chicken Run*'s chicken pies) in the world. And yet, despite everything stacked against me, I knew I wasn't going down without a fight. I began to make something of an action plan.

'Okay,' I grappled with myself, 'so I can't stop all of the bad things in the world from happening. Just because I can't single-handedly stop something I don't like doesn't mean that I have to be a part of it. I don't have to join in.' This felt like a pretty good compromise. So that was that. I opted out and, to this day, I have never eaten meat again. It seems dramatic now – to have such strong convictions at my young age – but it just made sense at the time. There was no way I was going to go anywhere near meat after that. After all, once I knew, how could I ever 'unknow' that information? People often ask what my parents thought and, especially now as an adult, I have a great deal of respect for the way that they handled their little girl making such a significant life decision. They later told me that they were certain it would just be a phase, and that I would grow out of it, but despite that they didn't try to persuade me otherwise or tell me that they knew better. And when I think about it now, who is to say that they *did* know better? Who is to say that we need to eat the flesh of others in order to survive? *Why couldn't we dare to think differently?* My parents, who still regard a meal without meat is incomplete, took me at my word as a seven-year-old. They simply set about ensuring that my diet had all the nutrients that a growing child required. I don't think it did me any harm. I am a healthy adult, filled with a zest for life. I find it fascinating to think now that one of my earliest memories – unbeknownst to me at the time – was the way in which food could become a means of making my own choices. It was a way of a small child standing up against the grain and, in her own small way, enacting change.

BUT I DON'T WANT TO EAT

I revelled in this sense of food as a means of standing up for my beliefs, as somehow being proof of the fact that I was *my own person*, for much of my childhood. I might have been young, but I do see that I became something of a zealot with it. Of course, the danger of engaging in food as a means of self-determination also meant that I ran the risk of it playing an overly important role in my very-much-still-developing identity formation. In giving it permission to form me, swept away in my drive to do what I believed to be right, I allowed myself to get lost in its flood. I was no longer a consumer. I was consumed.

I was eleven years old when I first decided to stop eating. 'Too large,' I decided. I don't need food. I'll just stop. Despite the tenuous connection I had made between food as sustenance / passion / play / political statement / joy, I was a child. And, sickeningly, this child had connected food with the (imagined) size of her thighs. Food became a battleground, a site of exhausting and seemingly never-ending ways to make my life difficult. It wasn't just my own life. My mother watched in silent concern as I refused the Friday-after-swimming chip-shop chips; a family tradition, previously my favourite. We were at a stalemate. I looked on, intrigued at my mother's furrowed brows and hushed conversations with teachers about the child who didn't want to eat. What to do with her? There weren't really any answers. I was as stubborn as they were concerned. I learnt to eat enough to placate them and not to affect my day-to-day activities. (I was a busy child, entranced by the world, and didn't want to actually eat so little that I had to stop *doing things*. Hospitalisation? No thank you very much.) Eventually, enticed by flavours and persuaded by the very real threat that if I didn't eat, I wouldn't grow, I got bored (or hungry) and moved on to the next thing – as children do. But I had formed a preoccupation with food that never really left me. I lived with disordered eating on and off for much of the next decade, periodically becoming quite dangerously thin – but never so much that it stopped me from *doing*. From then on, whether I was thinking about how *not* to eat, or delighting in the joys of my next meal, food in the very distinctive sense of its relationship to my own day-to-day was never far from my mind. 'So eating is growth,' I thought, pushing down the uncomfortable thought I had somewhere deep within that food could also be stasis.

It was only after leaving home and becoming personally responsible for my own nourishment that I began to see food not just as something that happened to me, affecting me without my permission, but rather as something that I could steer myself; a vehicle where I was in the driving seat. I think encountering food in this way requires an element of courage; of declaring a desire to discover and enter new worlds. It is also an arm outstretched to the power of storytelling, listening and looking between what we might have been told (or as-sumed so far) to find what actually makes us who we are. To love food is to love life. It is guttural and messy, lip-smacking and full-blooded; a clarion call for all who want to live boldly. Looking for the stories in the ingredients, the recipes and the sitting-down-to-eat is also a way of embracing that; of saying that the minutiae of day-to-day feels important, or even more than that: powerful.

I attended a talk recently that was looking at queer iden-tities and alternative ways of finding intimacy in the familial structure. It opened up a fascinating dialogue on what the family might look like if it was reframed away from het-eronormativity, individualism and the nuclear unit. There was much talk within this of the need to abolish the family, almost as the only way of achieving real, radical change. One of the panellists, scholar, writer and activist Lynne Segal, stepped in (rather brilliantly, in my mind) to point out that the simplistic idea that abolishing the family would solve all of the problems might not be as radical as it may initially appear. Many individuals don't have access to any other form of support network. Such a blanket ban risks ignoring each of these people, glossing over class, race and all of those groups and spaces where a welfare state doesn't exist, or isn't available – and where the family unit might be all that an individual feels that they have as a form of protection against external racism or poverty or any other prevailing factor. That is absolutely not to say that the family is perfect and without criticism, it is just to say that we can think bigger – more broadly – dream about more. If the traditional nuclear family unit doesn't work, then why don't we look elsewhere?

The kitchen and further practices around food are incredibly rich places to find evidence of wider family structures which do not fit that traditional nuclear model. The very act of sitting and sharing a meal is to create a bond; a community of sorts. More broadly speaking, food itself often exists at a community level and, as a community that is feeding and nurturing those within it, perhaps we can also see these bond groups as alternative family structures. We do not need to abolish the family. We just need to reframe how we look at it. We can cultivate change from within the very mechanisms of the institutions that we think are dragging us down. I take this thought and mull it over as I taste in my mouth the sharp tang of all those who spent their days in kitchens because they had no choice. But then, a softness, something that – maybe – if I just keep chewing, just keep working to separate the sweet from the sour, might become palatable – tasty, even.

When I was twenty, I moved to Paris and fell instantly in love; not with a person, but with the city, with the food – and with myself. Paris was the first place I felt I could truly call home. I became a woman in that city. It was a place of freedom, of independence – and a means of discovery that was intrinsically tied to food and exploring what the culture of food in France could mean to me, a girl from Northampton in the big city for the first time. Every Sunday I would set out from my apartment on the corner of the 3rd, 10th and 11th arrondissements and run down Boulevard Voltaire, feeling like the wind was pushing me along – as though I might fly. I would cross the Place de la Nation and head over through Bel-Air into the Bois de Vincennes before looping back and ending up at the Place de la Bastille, where my favourite food market was held each Sunday morning. I would savour every interaction – each moment – feeling impossibly grown up as I selected my fresh fruit and vegetables for the week ahead, swelling with pride that I could do something like negotiate the price of tomatoes in a language that was not my own. Once I had all that I needed for the coming week I would bundle my paper bags into the basket of a Vélib bicycle and ride back, stopping off at my favourite boulangerie for flaky croissants and coffee. Paris was dinner parties, picnics by the Seine, long lunches outside cafés and watching the world go by. It was my first adult heartbreak, first all-encompassing, knowing-every-single-minute-detail-about-each-other's-lives best friendship, first time exploring my sexuality, first time negotiating rent with landlords, first time going it alone, dreaming big and actually seeing a path for how to make things happen. I discovered what made me happy – what made my heart sing – and for the first time I got to do it all on my own terms. It is not lost on me that every single one of these experiences was accompanied by the tang of a silky-smooth Beaujolais, or a mouth-watering falafel wrap fresh from a little stall at the corner of Rue du Temple and Rue Rambuteau in the Marais.

At the other end of the spectrum, it was also the meticulous examination of my food for the meat that the uncomprehending Parisians insisted went into my vegetarian meals. There was little place in Paris for meals without meat and these were some of the rare moments where I felt conspicuously *foreign*, as though I had no sense of taste or understanding of what haute cuisine was supposed to be. I learnt to see the funny side – I sort of had to really, because otherwise I risked facing a dark truth: that I would never really integrate into Parisian communities when such a fundamental disconnect was woven into the fabric of its society. I was playing with the duality of food as a means of integration into a community that was not my own, while also furthering my own journey of self-discovery and identification through food and the place I was in – even when the two did not align. I became well-versed in menu checks and in emphasising in no uncertain terms '*Pas de poisson!*' (No fish!) but still found myself on many an occasion picking tuna chunks out of a salad, or, on one mortifying occasion, trying to remove meat from a risotto at a dinner party. I suppose I was always slightly on edge. But then I remember Bastille market and the boulangeries and the many glasses of *vin rouge*. My relationship with Paris is inseparable from my relationship with the food I ate there. It was alive and I came to life with it.

PARIS, OR:
FOOD IS ALSO LAUGHTER

I used to find it
Strange
Uncomfortable
Impossible
To tell people when they had cooked something I didn't like
Parisian dinner parties were the hardest
I remember one
Freezing cold apartment
Student living
Living
In the most beautiful city in the world
But couldn't put the heating on
And somehow this sweet kind girl
Who was hosting and cooking and sharing
with me
Had missed the memo that I thought
Meat was murder
She had cooked a risotto with all of the pieces of bacon left in
Lardons screaming at me

Loudly
NO
And instead of simply saying 'Oh I'm so
sorry but I'm actually vegetarian'
I picked around the lardons hoping to brave the
courage to put something into my mouth
But I couldn't and didn't because it was touching the meat
Same thing to me as an infectious disease
So I pretended
Picked around
So sorry
Not very hungry
Delicious though thank you
Thank you so much
(Making everything worse)
But when we got home we laughed
Til we cried
Put the heating on
And some frozen pizzas in the oven.

I learnt about myself by learning to cook. From the girl who had seen food as her enemy, then her joy, then a deep chasmic loss, a theft of something inexplicable that had been taken from her, it was also through food that I understood. It was through food that I reclaimed. It was through food that I became.

AUNT ESEEN

In 2014 I visited Jamaica for the first time, searching for –
something. I didn't know what. I had left Paris to spend a
summer working in Guadeloupe before island hopping a
little. Leaving was tumultuous. It felt like having a little
corner of my heart ripped out. Even now, any time I go back
and pass through my old neighbourhood it still feels like
a mild form of self-imposed torture. I thought getting to
Guadeloupe and the Caribbean might distract me and make
leaving Paris less painful but, while peppered with beautiful
moments, it was a lonely time.

When I first arrived, I was staying somewhere so remote
that the nearest shop was a six-mile drive away across moun-
tainous terrain. I didn't have a car. I also didn't have any
money at that point and was staying as a guest at the family
home of one of my colleagues from Paris. Not wanting to
impose any further than I felt that I already was, I found food
became a source of anxiety. I had no real means of being able
to do my own shop and I had not a penny to my name to do
anything about it, even if I wanted to. I was truly beholden to
my host family – but I already felt that they were doing too

much. As I began to feel more claustrophobic, isolated and lonely in Guadeloupe, my delight in the experience of food, so joyfully cultivated in Paris, faded away. I began to fade with it, becoming dangerously thin again. It wasn't an intentional thing. I just quite literally lost my appetite; for eating, for adventure – for whatever you want to call it. I wasn't hungry any more.

After a few months I left Guadeloupe, heading to Jamaica, where I was staying with my Aunt Eseen, a half-sister of my mother who I had only met once as a child. Arriving in the way that I did, I met her at my most vulnerable. Actually, if I think about it now, I can see that there was probably something liberating about having absolutely no expectations for my time there. I had nothing to prove. For the first time that summer, in a way that I hadn't experienced since I left Paris, I was ready to just e x i s t. On arrival I felt, almost immediately, a sense of grounding. My Aunt Eseen was quiet and measured. Thoughtful. We developed a mutual respect and understanding for each other's space, and I think she could tell that this was what I needed. She took me around the island, introducing me to family members and showing me my mother's country. Food was the centrepiece of our experiences every single time. Meeting family members out in the remote countryside and preparing meals to share together, the wonder of connecting for the first time was only enhanced by the flavours of the food and the love that would go into the preparation of it. Most of our relatives were elderly and very poor, so Aunt Eseen would bring fresh ingredients with us and distribute them in the no-nonsense way that she had. I will always remember my elderly great-aunt taking hold of my hand, eyes shining with tears. I paused, mid-way through preparing the vegetables, and looked up as she whispered to me that she thought she would die before ever meeting one of my granddad's 'grand pickney-dem'. The kitchen became a space where generational borders were broken, where anything could be said and where fleeting achingly beautiful memories were made. My great-aunt died not long after that trip, and the picture of me, her and my sister beaming with delight from the kitchen is one of my most treasured possessions.

Back at my Aunt Eseen's house I began to reflect more on what was able to happen in those sacred spaces and how food could unify us, even across generations and bloodlines and life experiences. She had a small but lovingly maintained garden. It was her great joy, and she grew almost everything there. I became infatuated with her mango tree. Just walking over and plucking a sweet succulent fruit from the branches, tucking into it like an apple, I delighted in the decadence of it, the innocence of it. Back home, the fruit that I encountered was presented to me: primed, plumped and preserved. I had to tear through packaging before I could even get to touch it and then it had to be pumped full of the preservatives needed to keep it looking exotic enough to pass muster. Here, it was different. I could as easily pluck and eat a mango as I could drink water or moisturise my skin. It felt nourishing.

One morning I came down to find my aunt kneading the dough to make dumplings as she did most days. 'Auntie,' I asked her, 'will you teach me to cook like you?' She nodded. 'Of course,' she said. Pleased in her own quiet way. And so we started a precious tradition of cooking classes in her kitchen. I learnt how to tell when the avocado was perfectly ripe, how to sauté callaloo with the best flavours and how to knead flour and water to make golden dumplings rise. It became something more than that though. I learnt to heal. In my aunt's kitchen no unwelcome ghoul could haunt me. No misintentioned friend could dim my light to make theirs shine brighter. As we laughed and moved about the kitchen – my simple questions, her precise answers, how much salt / how long in the oven / does this look right – it became a shared experience. We both rose and the higher I felt us lifting, the more I imagined others rising with me. As I blended blueberries, no cold-hearted person could use their force to bruise innocent skin that same colour. As I chopped ginger nobody could be told that they were too fiery or above their station. In the green of the callaloo I saw the expanse of a world opening up before me: places to be visited and things to be achieved. The changes *we* could cultivate in the world – magic to be made from our very own fingertips. Cooking showed me a whole new realm, glimmering with possibility. It was a freedom of sorts, the kind that I hadn't experienced before. But also, it was a sanctuary. In my aunt's kitchen I was safe. I could do anything, try anything, *be* anything. Being in her space was my key to learning about myself – and, just as importantly for me at that time, learning about my mother. It was a way in. And now, when I look at my family, I see the strength in them; the tower that they are building. My grandmother pretty much fed the entire elderly Caribbean community of Newport, South Wales until she was in her late eighties, stopping only when a global pandemic forced her hand. Cooking is her means of creating. The kitchen is the place where she is in control. She selects the dishes, she chooses the ingredients, she makes enough so that nobody goes without, she receives the gratitude from the satisfied mouths. It's her domain. It is a space of infinite possibility.

We can all do more to actively embrace the transformation that can happen in these spaces; the shifting of perspectives from what we typically associate with a very gendered – and powerless – space. Of course, history tells a tale of women who have been confined to the kitchen – and it is a beautiful thing to see them making a courageous escape for freedom from the shackles and drudgery of spatulas instead of schooling, and rotisserie instead of reaching for horizons new, but this really only paints the tiniest fraction of the picture. It also means that, for as long as we place shame on domestic spaces and categorise them as imprisoning certain groups somewhere that they don't want to be, we are also denying the opportunities for discovery that surround them. What if we embraced those shimmering possibilities, removed the boundaries and just let the flavours ring out?

FRIED DUMPLINGS

Self-raising flour
Pinch of salt
Knob of margarine (optional)
Cold water
Sunflower oil, for frying

My mama:

Put flour, salt and margarine into a bowl. Mix in margarine to get outer crunchy texture. Pour in a little bit of water at a time and knead together until it looks like dough. Once that's done, put it to the side. Pour cooking oil into a frying pan or saucepan. Heat it until it is hot. While oil is heating, break off a little bit of dough at a time and roll it in the palm of hands until it looks like a dough ball. Once done, put it into the hot oil to fry. Turn down the heat to prevent it burning on the outside and not cooking on the inside. Cook for about 15 minutes. Once cooked, place it into an ovenproof dish and keep warm until all the dumplings have been cooked.

Me:

Knead flour, salt and water in a bowl by hand. I find this easier than my sister Hannah because her hands are clammy. But her dumplings still probably taste better. Roll the balls of dough into circles. Put oil into a frying pan and place the balls of dough in. I always sprinkle a little salt over the top at this point for good measure. Fry until golden.

PART II

RUPTURE

Main course
noun

The principal dish of a meal.

Where we break down in order to rebuild.

SHE WROTE IT DOWN

The practice of creating and consuming food is part of a shared history that we carry with us today. Its scent wafts out of our kitchen windows and seeps under the doors of our neighbours, trailing its way back through time to the feet of our ancestors and forward to us today, clinging to our hair and our skin. We owe it to our ancestors to stir their names into the dish we are cooking up; not just from the kitchen but from right across the process of cultivating and preparing food. Food, food practices and the crafting of worlds in kitchens are not new. If we look closely, an acknowledgement of what has gone before can help us in both seeking and finding answers for what might come next. As I discovered that summer in my Aunt Eseen's kitchen, these practices are part of an intricately woven lineage that dates back alongside any other form of history, right through generations all the way to our 'grandmothers'.

Recipes, both the carefully curated, formal collections that we see in books and the word-of-mouth 'my grandmother always does it like this' kind, are filled with expansive possibilities around food ringing out in surprising places. If we look back, we can take clues from them and use them to propel us forward in building communities, forming identities and creatively experimenting with 'writing' our stories. These 'grandmothers' – our ancestors – were massively creative in the kitchen but didn't get to share their artistry with the world. Between the eighteenth and the twentieth centuries, an estimated 100,000 recipe collections made it into print but fewer than two hundred were credited to Black cooks and writers, despite the presumed figures being much higher. This might seem inconsequential. After all, what have recipe collections got to do with taking us forward? In fact, the opposite has historically been true. Recipes have been an archaic way of memorialising food, of following instructions to the letter and, as artefacts that have historically been written by, marketed towards and catered to women, they have also been a way of enforcing outdated gender binaries. Identifying as a woman does not have to mean nurturing, nursing and caring. In wanting to seek out a progressive and empowering narrative around marginalised groups who have typically been locked away in the kitchen, the tendency has been to shun recipes and cookbooks as being products of a laborious and complex history of subjugation. I dare us to think differently. I won't argue with the fact that the publication of collections of recipes upholds and feeds into elements of patriarchy, capitalism and traditional structures. However, is it possible that it could also be something more? We stand to miss out on a lot if we don't at least try to look deeper. It would, in theory, be easy to see the key to successful cooking as following a series of instructions: mix x with y and cook at a certain heat for a specific length of time. And yet, that is to miss the nuances of the in-between. For so many of our ancestors, recipes move far beyond simply citing instructions. They are steeped in cultural legacy, fusing food with the generational nuances of our creativity. What a waste of potentially precious resources if we continue today to let the insights of these creators go uncredited and unacknowledged. The laughter that resides in the middle of adding the yeast and allowing the dough to rise. The grit and determination baked into its crust. The ingredients and stages in creating these dishes are our blueprint and often a key to a history that has not been documented. In the dish that we are cooking up, they imbue our complex histories with a richness that makes it smooth to the taste.

What if, instead, while acknowledging that recipes are artefacts of a particular time when the kitchen was a place of unpaid labour and servitude – and even acknowledging that in so many ways this is still the case – we also see the possibility of imagining otherwise? There is something quietly revolutionary about seeing some of the early cookbooks and recipes that we can access as treasure troves, used by their creators as scrapbooks where they documented their lives for those who came after them, with food often being a window into their own worlds. Through cookbooks, these women wrote themselves into existence, taking stories told on a veranda, at special occasions, while working together or by feeding a family, and then preserving them for future generations. Yes, they are a means of upholding patriarchy, but they are also a space of radical change with extraordinary consequences.

Recipes, if we are prepared to think differently when we look at them, provide a place for resistance and creativity to meet head on. Instead of inhibiting us, stifling us as we place them in the oven, just stop and watch them bubble and rise. Look. Out comes something golden. A community of individuals, passing their secrets on; a different kind of family. It is a family that is vast in its circulatory reach. Just think how far recipes travel. They are passed across time, space and circumstance. The likelihood is that they may go further than their creator could ever even dream of for themselves. This circulatory potential, coupled with the fact that recipes are often overlooked as political tools, is electric. They are texts, imbued with all of the potency that the written word possesses, but they are also blueprints for a way of living. That, I think, makes them radical. It makes them subversive.

Smart-Grosvenor continues to solidify this idea for me in *Vibration Cooking: Or, The Travel Notes of a Geechee Girl*. Recipes can travel – and *we can carry them*. She dedicates her book 'to my mama and grandmothers and my sisters in appreciation of the years that they have worked in miss ann's kitchen and then came home to TCB [take care of business] in spite of slavery and the moynihan report [*sic*]'.* I think again of that talk I attended and the call to abolish the family. As if she knew that I needed to hear from her, Smart-Grosvenor is talking to me, showing me an example of a family unit that sustains and maintains outside of the traditional nuclear model. It enables other women to go further. Smart-Grosvenor is showing me that cooking is alive – and it is providing alternative means for intergenerational survival. She's taking care of business, all right. Carrying it on her back as we join her in taking radical steps forward.

---

* A 1965 report on Black poverty in the United States.

PAP FOR INFANT DIET

Take one pint of flour, sift it and tie it up in a clean cloth securely tight, so that no water can get into it; and put it in boiling water and let it boil steady for two hours, then take it out of water, and when it gets cold take outside crust from it. Whenever you are ready to nurse or feed the child, grate one tablespoon of the boiled flour, and stir it into half a pint of boiled milk while the milk is boiling; sweeten the same with white sugar to taste. When the child has diarrhea, boil a two-inch stick of cinnamon in the pap. I have given birth to eleven children and raised them all, and nursed them with this diet.[1]

This little scrap of knowledge imparted – part recipe, part instruction, part personal story – comes from Abby Fisher, a formerly enslaved cook who went on to live a bold and courageous life, never for one minute allowing her situation to prevent her from using any means she could to uplift herself and her family. We know very little about her, but what we do know, which I love, we have gleaned from what she left behind for us through food.

Her 1881 *What Mrs Fisher Knows About Old Southern Cooking* is one of the earliest cookbooks written by an African American woman, second only to Malinda Russell's more well known 1866 *Domestic Cook Book: Containing a Careful Selection of Useful Receipts for the Kitchen*. However, while Russell's cookbook sings out a song of freedom with its cosmopolitan recipes, Fisher's (published over fifteen years later) hums a different melody: stoic, more resilient. Perhaps unsurprisingly with Fisher, who, notably, unlike Russell, had not been born a free woman, her recipes have an element of the practical at their core. In Fisher's own words, they are born from 'her experience of upwards of thirty-five years – in the art of cooking'. Her recipes are resourceful; the sort that keep families together and young mouths fed. The sort that keep histories, legacies and communities alive. Her cookbook is a way of ensuring that a world that was communicated primarily orally (food and food practices) would not die along with those who had the knowledge of the recipes. She brought to life recipes for different preserves, pickles and jams, and went on to become well known for them. She calls her blackberry syrup an 'old Southern plantation home remedy among colored people' – a bringing to the light of the food practices of her people and the ways that they looked after each other, while also giving an insight into the personal. Most personal of all – her recipe that endlessly fascinates me – is her 'pap for infant diet'.

The 'pap' – a sort of porridge-like dish made from grains cooked in water – is a nod to Fisher's days of being enslaved but also, more crucially, to her survival. She seamlessly fuses recipe with anecdote as she discloses how she has birthed, raised and nursed all eleven of her children with this diet. Her simple instructions are so direct and clear that I feel like I can almost hear her voice as I read her recipe for keeping her babies alive. It is an extraordinary claim of survival; the right to ensure that her babies *lived*. In the nineteenth-century context in which Fisher was writing, infant mortality rates were high. The idea that children wouldn't survive to adulthood was the norm – expected, even. Abby Fisher rejected this, declaring that, against all odds, her children would *survive*. More than that though: in the nineteenth century, when Black women frequently worked as nannies and mammies, raising white children before they went home to care for their own, Abby Fisher's recipe storms into a staunch declaration. Not only has she given birth to eleven children, but she has also gone on to nurse and raise them all herself. What could so easily have been overlooked as a tiny little note in a recipe book becomes a proud self-declaration of a laudable set of skills and accomplishments both as a cook and as a mother. 'Goodbye,' she says to the image of Black women being made to look after white children. 'Not today,' she says to the notion that a formerly enslaved person might not be in control of their own destiny. This innocuous little recipe for infant milk so pointedly placed at the close of Abby Fisher's recipe book undermines both of these stereotypes placed on Black women, instead drawing attention to the fact that not only are they women, wives, mothers and individuals in their own right, but they are gifted, creative and talented cooks, in full command of their own kitchens. I can't help but read Fisher's publishing a book that acknowledges her hardships and then, within the very lines of the recipes, holding her head high and declaring that she has kept eleven children alive despite what life has thrown at her, as a most courageous rupturing of all expectations. It is a quiet, resourceful revolution. We move through so that we can move beyond.

I wonder what made Fisher decide to document her recipes in the first place, especially given that, having spent much of her life enslaved, she could not read or write. It is hard not to tune in to the dark echo of slavery that is present throughout the book. Fisher fairly frequently mentions that certain recipes were born out of a life on the Southern plantation she had left behind. With slavery existing as such a lingering presence, I can't help but ask: whose voice are we actually hearing? Sometime after the end of the civil war, Fisher moved away from the South towards San Francisco with her family, and started up a pickle business that went on to be a lucrative project for her. It seems that it was at some point while she was out west that her pickle business caught the attention of whoever it was that ended up helping her formally publish a cookbook.

This becomes even more interesting when you think about what it means in terms of who is actually in possession of power. Power dynamics, essentially the balance – or lack of – between two or more people, underpin everything that we do, every relationship that we have and also dictate the way that we carry ourselves and move through the world. They are implicit in every single interaction and experience, with food being no exception. What is seen as palatable is decided upon. Who has access to it is a political act. These things do not just happen. They do not just exist. There is no 'neutral'. Neutral is a battleground. The questions we need to be asking ourselves are *who* gets to make these decisions? Who drives the direction of the warfare?

I was made distinctly aware of how power dynamics shape each of our interactions with food on a trip to Nigeria, while out for dinner with my friend Samuel. I realised that the vegetarian options on the menu were extremely limited. I asked the waiter what I might be able to eat and she smiled at me before turning to Samuel and explaining that for vegetarians they could do rice and a vegetable stew. I thanked her for the options and confirmed that I would have both. She smiled at me again before looking at Samuel and asking him if I wanted the rice and the stew to arrive at the same time. I confirmed that yes I did. She thanked Samuel for my order and left. When my food arrived shortly later, the vegetable stew had meat in it. I didn't eat it, thankfully spotting the animal flesh long before it met my lips, but I felt the pain of it; all the more so because it somehow seemed as though the options for me to communicate about what I wanted had been taken from me. The process of explaining about the meat was laborious, and at some point in the interaction it finally dawned on Samuel too that my gender in that interaction precluded me from being able to effectively communicate – or perhaps rather to be listened to. Eventually, I bit my lip and kept quiet, knowing even before it happened that the bill would be placed in front of Samuel, that he would pay. I assumed the role of docile, fragile woman. Then I got in my Uber and sent Samuel a bank transfer.

In the case of Abby Fisher, these power dynamics were even more complicated, dictated by her gender, her race and her social status. Right up until the very recent years before publishing her cookbook, Fisher was owned. She was answerable to white folk and, especially in the domestic setting, to white women. The power dynamic was not skewed in her favour. By bringing out her cookbook in this context, Fisher turns these power dynamics on their head. In this scenario, by having the key to bringing together healthy, nutritious and delicious ingredients, the Black woman has something that the white woman wants, and she is willing to give it to her, for a fee. More than just the courage that this must have taken, it was also a shrewd financial move. There is bravery in Fisher's cookbook, but there is also a disruption of the dynamics that would have kept her down. Her drive to take the hardships that life had given her and turn them into something that would bring growth is quietly radical; a tribute to the sorrows brought to her without ever denying the pain that they had caused. Power is not absolute. It too can be transformed.

I want to take this as a blueprint for how to look at food in a different way. Abby Fisher and her cookbook are the perfect example of how recipes are more than just a series of instructions. They teach us how we can use food to bring the past into the present and shine a light on where women have been creating / recreating / challenging the bitter tang of the constructed ideal. Through them, we become collaborators in the reworking and reimagining of the power dynamic that we have been handed. Through them, we can take our hardships and press them down, squeezing until we create something new: the sweetness of lemonade. More than that though. My every thought brings me back to the fact that I could be drawing such inspiration from a woman who lived many years before I was born. I see myself through the eyes of my grandmother – and then in the image of the women who had gone before her, tracing their activism all the way back in the hope that it might help us to move forward; going back in order to go beyond As well as actively using food to uplift herself, Abby Fisher also reframed the paradigm for every single person coming after her, raising valid questions around authorship as well as ownership – of everything from land to personhood to ideas and who has the right to access what. We are accountable to our ancestors. We owe it to them to keep alive the history that they so diligently set out for us; to rewrite the history that hasn't done them justice but also, crucially, to go beyond it. We owe it to them to write new stories. That we are now able to look at recipes from over one hundred years ago and find a connection to ourselves is extraordinary. That words can leap from a page and become a blueprint for us to learn more about our own abilities – see our own strength (and that of each other) – is emboldening. It makes me think more about the power of the pen, and why our words matter. We consume words too.

PIGS

I mull over the links between the process of crafting recipes and that of writing our stories. If there is power in the pen, then it stands to reason that there is a powerful – political – nuance to what we consume, and the process of preparing it for consumption too. Fannie Lou Hamer, a civil rights activist born in 1917 to sharecroppers in Montgomery County, Mississippi, saw revolution through the language of food and the folklore of the land. Cotton, labour, animals, food – these were the parameters that she knew, the landscapes of her world. And, when she saw that it was required, when her world was under threat, she rose up to protect them. In the early 1960s this time came.

Despite Black people representing 50 per cent of Mississippi's voting-age population, they were entirely unrepresented politically. In 1964 Jamie Whitten, chairman of the House Appropriations Subcommittee on Agriculture, was seeking his thirteenth term. When he had previously been elected in 1962, only 31,345 people voted, despite there being over 300,000 people of voting age in the district (a population that was 59 per cent Black).

Many of the most well-known civil rights activists of the time, such as Martin Luther King Jr, were taking this to task through organised and powerful means of protest. Hamer, an uneducated cotton picker from the Mississippi Delta, might not seem like the obvious person to do something about this; however, in August 1964, she stepped up to the challenge of passionately demanding the right to represent Mississippi citizens as a party delegate. Her modus operandi? Her knowledge of food and the land.

In a 1964 interview with the *Nation*, she explains how her goal was to wake up the citizens of her district by 'showing people that a Negro can run for office' and citing perhaps her most famous phrase: that she was 'sick and tired of being sick and tired'.[2] I breathe deeply, willing my imagination to take me back to that courtroom, to bring me to a place that I have never been. Back through my mind I go to the crevices of my imagination and the place where, in 1965, Hamer brought *Hamer v. Campbell*, a civil rights case against Cecil Campbell, the circuit clerk of Mississippi, for denying her and other Black people the right to register and vote.

I imagine myself an observer in that room, listening intently as, taking to the witness table, Hamer draws a deep breath. She looks up, taking in row upon row of people – men – who stare back, unamused and unimpressed. It is hot in the room and Hamer feels sweat beading, pooling, then trickling. She is up after two of her male colleagues, both of whom read from their pre-prepared statements, barely looking up. It is ... uninspiring to say the least. The room feels heavy with the tedium of their words. How could they have expected anyone to be moved – inspired – by that? Fannie Lou Hamer knows what she must do. She points her chin, raises her gaze to the two hundred or so spectators and reporters and decides that she has nothing to lose. She must speak.

From the soul, Fannie's voice rings out. Tremoring at first, she explains how as sharecroppers farming cotton they are unable to break out of the never-ending cycle of poverty. To cover the costs of animals for labour, food, seed, equipment and housing, they have to borrow money from their landlord at highly inflated prices, only to repeat the cycle all over again.

It's just existing. Not really living. Existing ...

We went back to sharecroppin', halvin', it's called. You split the cotton half and half with the plantation owner. But the seed, fertilizer, cost of hired hands, everything is paid out of the cropper's half.

Later, I dropped out of school. I cut corn stalks to help the family. My parents were getting on in age – they weren't young when I was born. I was the twentieth child ...

So many times for dinner we would have greens with no seasonin' ... and flour gravy. My mother would mix flour with a little grease and try to make gravy out of it. Sometimes she'd cook a little meal and we'd have bread.

No one can honestly say Negroes are satisfied. We've only been patient, but how much more patience can we have?[3]

It is the simplicity of her statements that enthrals me, reading this now. Food is the key to a life fully and bodily experienced, but in the same breath it is also a means of simply existing; a life never fully realised. I wonder if there is also something about what she was saying that resonated with those listening who had never had to work with the land in order to survive. I come back again to the role that power plays. As long as the landlord continues inflating the prices the same system can never be escaped from. This is at a financial level, but as Hamer continues to speak it becomes clearer that the body can be stripped of its power too.

Growing in confidence, Hamer describes how she was sterilised against her will by a white doctor while undergoing a routine appendectomy – and how this bid to put an end to poor Black women reproducing is so common that it is simply known as 'the Mississippi appendectomy'. Desperate to become a mother, not to let this dream be wrenched from her, she adopted two daughters with her husband only for their landlord to evict them, simply because she tried to register to vote.

> My oldest girl met me and told me that Mr. Marlowe, the plantation owner, was mad and raisin' Cain. He had heard that I had tried to register. That night he called on us and said, 'We're not ready for that in Mississippi now. If you don't withdraw, I'll let you go.' I left that night but 'Pap' – that's what I call my husband – had to stay on till work on the plantation was through.[4]

Again the process of sharecropping, of working with the harvest to cultivate the food that will keep her and her family alive, is also shown to be the site of subjugation. To the spellbound convention room in Atlantic City, Hamer speaks louder, clearer now, telling of the state-sanctioned police beatings, the sexual assaults and the four days of imprisonments because she tried to help other people register to vote. I struggle to carry on reading, such is the brutal nature of the assaults.

President Lyndon Johnson, listening in live on television, is so concerned about the potential backlash from Hamer's heartbreaking testimony that he calls a press conference, hoping to stop cameras broadcasting Hamer's speech to the nation. Hamer is unperturbed, alive with confidence now and knowing that she has the audience if not on her side then at least willing to listen. They hear her cry. Ending her impassioned eight-minute speech, she pleads to the room: 'Is this America, the land of the free and the home of the brave, where ... our lives be threatened daily, because we want to live as decent human beings, in America?'

For Hamer, the right to vote was as innate – as essential – as the right to breathe, or to eat. Her work on the land was being denied to her, but so was her fundamental right as a citizen to have a say in how her country was governed. Working with food and the land was what she did; what she knew. Her access to food ownership was as vital to her as her more obviously political rights such as the right to vote. One form of power is inextricably linked to the other. It is these power structures themselves that we need to disrupt. Failure to do so is a denial of the most fundamental of human rights; a total oppression that left Hamer feeling 'sick and tired of being sick and tired' – and, just like Abby Fisher before her, determined to rise up and lift as many others with her as she could. As part of her voter-registration work, she also taught citizenship classes, working to provide a decent level of schooling for Black children. Mississippi had no compulsory school-attendance law; it was abolished after the 1954 Supreme Court school-desegregation decision. Many Black children did not attend school because they were working, picking cotton out in the fields. For others it was as simple as the fact that they had no clothes to wear. Hamer helped organise clothing sent down from the North and distributed it among those who needed it. Even with the actual distribution process, Hamer cleverly combined the essentials of getting clothes on people's backs with encouraging voter activism, telling people that if they registered to vote they wouldn't have to wait in line to collect their clothes – a genius plan. Speaking to the *Nation*, she stated: 'We owe a lot to people in the North . . . a lot of people are wearing nice clothes for the first time. A lot of kids couldn't go to school otherwise.'[5] Eventually, the Fifth Circuit Court of Appeals ruled that Hamer and others were discriminated against by being denied the right to register to vote. The elections were then overturned based on discriminatory election practices. Hamer's work contributed in part to the Voting Rights Act being passed in 1965, making it illegal to deny any adult US citizen their right to vote and guaranteeing federal protection to ensure that this would not be thwarted. It sounds familiar. I think of Georgia native Stacey Abrams who led a crusade against voter suppression ahead of the 2020 US election and registered 800,000 voters in Georgia, 45 per cent of whom were under the age of thirty and 49 per cent of the global majority.[6]

Being able to actively trace these connections between women who were on a crusade to ensure equitable access to fundamental rights, from Fisher to Hamer to Abrams, shows how food is not just a means of survival or of identity formation, but also a community-driven political catalyst. From there, Hamer went on to found the Freedom Farm Cooperative in 1969, buying 40 acres of land for families around her to own and farm collectively, growing vegetables, soybeans and cotton. This was followed by a pig bank to provide free pigs for Black farmers to breed, raise and slaughter. The importance of these initiatives cannot be overstated. In cultivating a space for Black communities to create their own food production mechanisms and make money from them, a possibility that had been systemically denied to them by the US government (as Hamer had proven from her court case), the Freedom Farm Cooperative did exactly what it said on the tin: it allowed Black families to become self-sufficient – and cultivate their own freedom. Once these support systems were in place, the community could more effectively participate and lead in other forms of protest and activism. Ultimately, what Hamer did was create a blueprint for the modern protest movements around food. Just like Abby Fisher before her, she created the space for survival. I start to see more signs of the political. Food for Hamer was sovereignty. It was staking claim to something that should be a given – something that is not up for negotiation. Food is our weapon here and we raise it, sharpen it. Food becomes the symbol – the catalyst – to inspire change. But, it is also an end goal, an objective in and of itself: food was both the means of and result of a drive to bring about equality. Ultimately, what Hamer showed us was how food could be freedom.

DRIVING RESISTANCE

I take this realisation and I float, I feel buoyed, even more motivated to continue uncovering the stories of our ancestors, looking for further evidence of how things have been – and what we can take from the foundations they have laid in order to move ourselves forward. This search pulls me in surprising directions. I discover that there is a house in Montgomery, Alabama that is about five minutes away from where Martin Luther King Jr. and his family lived. On the outside of the house, so nondescript that if you didn't know you were looking for it you might even miss it, is a plaque that reads: 'Georgia Gilmore ... a solid and energetic boycott participant and supporter.' Intrigued, I begin to look further. Who was this woman? I find out that Gilmore was an Alabaman whose grass-roots activism and fundraising helped sustain the 382-day-long Montgomery bus boycott that was a large part of the eventual success of the civil rights movement. In her seventy years, Gilmore also worked as a midwife, a cook, a domestic worker and even on the railroads. I revisit the inscription on her house; the all-too-brief summary of an entire life. 'Solid and energetic.' I mean ... sure.

I want to go deeper though. I need to go deeper. I need to know what else there is.

Before the bus boycott, as racial tensions were increasing across Alabama, food became even more potent than ever; both a fuel for and a weapon in the fight for civil rights. The Jim Crow laws that kept white and Black people apart in almost all public spaces were at their most rigid where food was concerned. Gilmore worked as a cook at Montgomery's National Lunch Counter, where she and a team of mostly Black cooks prepared Southern specialities before white servers passed them to the diners – with a seven-foot-high partition to keep Black and white diners separate. This partition was replicated in her journey to and from work each day, where she was forced to sit at the back of the bus to be kept separate from white patrons. In October 1954, Gilmore was making the two-mile journey to work and went to sit at the back as usual. She was looking for a seat, preparing for the long and gruelling day ahead of her carrying out harsh physical labour, when the bus driver shouted at her for using the front door. The rule at the time, embedded in the segregationist Jim Crow laws, was that Black passengers would pay their fare at the front, disembark and enter the bus from the back door in order to take a seat. I am certain that Gilmore was simply tired and had entered from the front by accident. In her own words, she immediately realised her mistake and disembarked. However, as she went to the back door to get on, the driver drove away. Humiliating. And cruel too. My heart aches for her. Later in interviews she speaks about how 'I would always ask the Lord if it would ever be – become possible – for me to be able to just go around and not have to worry about going in the back door or getting up, giving somebody else my seat.'[7] Perhaps unsurprisingly, Gilmore had already taken the decision to boycott the Montgomery buses before the official protests began. Less than a year after that, following the infamous arrest of Rosa Parks, the boycott became official.

On 5 December 1955, just four days after Parks's refusal to stand, Dr King addressed the people of Holt Street Baptist Church, sparking the Montgomery bus boycott, a year-long movement that not only ended segregation on Montgomery buses but also stimulated activism and participation from the South in the civil rights movement at a national level, bringing the attention of the entire country to Dr King as a rising leader in the process. But back to that December day in 1955. Church – and a growing feeling of unrest lingering in the air like embers from the fire, or steam from the pan of boiling water, condensing now on the windows, dripping down. Here to stay. Still stinging with embarrassment and frustration from her own experiences with the Montgomery buses, Gilmore approached Dr King and introduced herself, joining the movement known as the Montgomery Improvement Association (MIA) on the spot and offering up her services. She knew that the front lines weren't an option for her – she needed to hold down her job and support her family – but one thing she did know was how to cook. And that was precisely what Georgia Gilmore did.

If one of the goals of these segregationist laws was to stop community from forming, food existed as one of the biggest threats to their implementation, doing nothing but showcasing quite how powerful it actually was. As the MIA began to strategise and the boycott got started, Gilmore set to work. She recruited other women from church and from the community around her to cook. They started selling delicious fried chicken sandwiches outside the church where meetings were taking place. They sold these sandwiches at every single mass meeting, providing their own home-cooked wares to feed the movers and the shakers – and then used the finances to fund the movement. I cannot stress the importance of this enough. The bus boycott needed every bit of support in order to quite literally get people from A to B. If people didn't have a means of getting where they needed to go, then the movement risked failure. The funds raised by Gilmore and her team of cooks helped to fund alternative means of transport – the carpool system that became the backbone of the movement – to ensure that people could get to their destinations. She named her movement the Club from Nowhere to preserve the anonymity of the members as well as contributors (some of whom were white). When she was dismissed from the lunch company where she worked, Dr King and other leaders of the MIA helped her to set up a restaurant in her home as a way for her to make a living. With a dining room as well, Gilmore's place became a community hub where Dr King and other members of the MIA would sit, strategise, recoup and organise. Members of the club would bake pies and cakes for sale to people of all races. Hundreds of people passed through her house, filled with both a hunger for her cooking and for political change. Cooking was not just a tool to fill the bellies and fuel the movement. Instead, it actually provided the hard funds needed to make it all possible. It gave the movement practical credibility. Here, food itself is the movement, and Gilmore is a driving force.

It was also a respite from the cruel world outside. Where fear lingered in the air out there, Gilmore cooked up relief. She stirred in shelter. Even the name of the club was interesting. When people would ask where the money came from, Gilmore and the fellow members would respond 'nowhere'. Nobody was going to risk bringing harm on themselves or their families by supporting the movement. More than that though, it also evokes a sense of community cohesion. It wasn't about one particular individual, but rather a collective, bringing together resources and passion. It was a place where food joined forces with network building to become a resistance of the highest order. With Gilmore helming the cooking club and overseeing bake sales, as well as attending weekly church services (which were also community meetings) and filling hampers with food to sell to both Black and white Alabamans (some of whom, in a delightful twist, didn't realise they were directly supporting the boycott), it was a thriving set-up. Civil rights strategy meetings took place over plates of mac and cheese and pies and the Club from Nowhere was frequently bringing in as much as $600 a week. Feeding a family, elevating a community and also funding a movement. It is a radical revolution.

For Gilmore and her cooking contemporaries, their work in the kitchen never meant the promise of equality; equality wasn't really a viable goal (in the short term anyway), for there were too many hurdles to overcome. They were still tucked away in the kitchen as opposed to being out there in the heart of the action. However, it did mean small blocks of change that laid great foundations. It meant uniting a group, the promise of income, funding a movement. It took what had been a skill set entirely co-opted by the dominant forms of power and flipped it on its head, making it a means of supporting the self and the community.

Georgia Gilmore and her contemporaries had taken things further, showing how food itself could not only inspire change but could actively exist as the driving force behind a political movement. Now let us consider food not just as the force behind activism but as the lifeblood of the movement itself. By viewing food as a crusade and paying tribute to the food activists who have paved the way, what might we begin to understand about the world we live in today? I dive deeper still, searching for answers in the history of food as a weapon of protest. What can I take from it to understand how I might effectively strategise and mobilise as an activist moving forward?

I search again, feeling that I am on the cusp of piecing something together but not quite sure how to play my next move – or even what I am looking for. I am fascinated by these examples of women as soldiers, and yet never being the face of the fight. I find myself back at Georgia Gilmore and her army of women. Who, or what, came next? In fact, more than a decade after the Club from Nowhere's galvanising, ground-breaking work we can see the ripple effect of food as a potent weapon in the armoury of activism continuing.

The Black Panther Party, initially founded by college students Bobby Seale and Huey P. Newton in October 1966 to put an end to police brutality, introduced the Free Breakfast for

School Children Program that went on to become one of the party's central activities. Not dissimilar to the mayor of London's free school meals for primary school children initiative introduced in 2023–4, the Black Panther programme ensured that all school-aged children were fed before each day of school. The programme didn't have any official funding and operated almost entirely on community cooperation and action. It was quite simple: party members and volunteers would visit local grocery stores and persuade generous owners to donate items such as grits, eggs, bread and milk. They would then work with nutritionists to curate healthy breakfast options for children, before congregating in church kitchens to prepare and serve nutritious meals to the young, hungry mouths free of charge. By making sure that Black children were starting their school day well fed, the Panthers were quite literally feeding the bodies and minds of the next generation. Food was an active means of radical action, becoming a way of the Panthers holding the government to account, while also ensuring that Black children did not fall behind because of the government's ineptitude. By pointing to how solving hunger could also solve societal issues, we see an incendiary indictment of the role that food plays as a means of inciting radical change too. It was a different – and particularly potent – form of revolution.

It brings me circling back again to those wider questions around food access, which, at the time of the programme being established, was failing. The US government had pledged a war on poverty, promising to provide basic needs for its citizens. In reality, those basic rights of food, housing, employment and safety were not being extended to Black citizens and the Panthers' programme shed important light on the gaps in what the US government had in place. The Panthers started the Free Breakfast Program because hunger and poverty made it difficult for many poor Black children to concentrate in school. In 1968, most of these children went to school hungry and stayed hungry. The national School Lunch Program provided reduced-price, but not free, lunches for poor children, and the national School Breakfast Program was limited to a few rural schools. Black children were arriving at school starving, falling asleep in class, and quite simply were unable to get the most out of their education.

Jocelyn Jackson is a co-founder of People's Kitchen Collective, an initiative started in Oakland in 2007 to continue the Panthers' legacy by creating food experiences that inspire people to reconnect with themselves, the earth and one another with the goal of collective liberation. Jackson (who also, beautifully, starts every meal with a song) speaks compellingly about the trailblazing scheme:

> Our society is not going to support our existence. They would actually prefer if we faded away. So in that moment, what are we going to do? The Black Panthers, they said we will provide ... This was a moment of yes from our past that we want to be in our present. And so we will do that year after year after year. We will be in that park that has so much history of bringing our community together and say every year: we want you to survive.[8]

What is fascinating to me as I read her words, praise for the mayor of London's similar objective to offer primary school children free lunches very much in my mind, is that the Black Panthers' programme, which so evidently inspired movements throughout history, was received by the authorities with outright animosity. It doesn't seem like something that it should be possible to criticise, but authority figures at the time certainly managed. Then director of the FBI J. Edgar Hoover called it 'the greatest threat to efforts by the authorities'.[9] At his instruction, FBI agents knocked on doors across the country to tell parents that the programme was a means of indoctrinating their children with racist Black Panther Party ideology. At one school in Chicago, police raided the makeshift kitchen, destroying the food and urinating on it.

'One of our primary aims in counterintelligence as it concerns the [Black Panther Party] is to keep this group isolated from the moderate black and white community which may support it,' Hoover wrote on 27 May 1969.[10] 'This is most emphatically pointed out in their Breakfast for Children Program, where they are actively soliciting and receiving support from uninformed whites and moderate blacks.'[11] By November, the Panthers reported that the programme had spread to twenty-three cities. Between 1969 and 1970, the party claimed to have distributed free breakfast to 20,000 children. It was a real and present threat to the government, and Hoover was afraid because the programme ran the risk of gaining support from both the liberal white and moderate Black folk who would otherwise have seen the Panthers as an extreme terrorist organisation. By operating in the space of community organisation and survival, the Panthers actually employed their most impressive method of recruitment, declaring to the population en masse that they were not just aggressive men with fists raised, holding a gun. Rather, they were actually doing the government's work for them. It was a stroke of genius.

This doesn't mean that the programme was without its issues. Look closer at who was actually helping to present this image of respectability and over and over again you will find the women of the movement.

I trawl through interviews with some of these women and a surprising pattern emerges. They were teachers, organisers, leaders, you name it – but often absolutely *not* cooks. There are some rather brilliant interviews with ex-members laughing at the fact that they were not all skilled in the kitchen, but rather motivated individuals who just wanted to further the cause, laughing about their cooking mishaps – egg shells in fried eggs and overcooked food. Yes, ostensibly this is amusing, but it also raises for me the very real question of *why* these women, brilliant activists in their own right, were resigned to the kitchens when, by their own admissions, they were not skilled and talented chefs. There was absolutely nothing in them that made them any more predisposed to being the ones to do the cooking except for the fact of their gender.

I sit with this slightly uncomfortable thought. I know that the Panthers had some of the most formidable activists of our time, including Afeni Shakur (mother of the rapper Tupac), Elaine Brown, who eventually rose to be chair of the party, and Assata Shakur, who lives in exile in Cuba and is still listed by the FBI as one of its most wanted 'terrorists'. And yet, when the kitchen was the war room of the movement it was women who were brought in to work there. Of course,

these kitchens were extremely effective politically, but still
it was the women who *had* to do this work. It just doesn't
quite feel right, despite the fact that nobody would argue
with the suggestion that these women were the heart of the
movement, vital in enacting genuine change. What does it
mean, then, for the kitchen to emerge as a space of both oppression and of liberation? Well, I suppose it means coming
back again to our understanding – and redefining – of power
structures. We have to recognise the power that lies in the
kitchen. It is a space of urgent potency; so urgent, in fact,
that it represented a threat to the government of the United
States. The fact that we haven't traditionally seen it as such
is not because this is anything new but rather because of the
way that power has been situated. For those who have existed
in societal roles that have been more powerfully positioned,
the kitchen has been a means of reinforcing those positions.
It is in their interests to keep those whose skill sets lie within
the food system down. Do not forget that. Food is not a trifle.
Food is an urgent, essential battleground. It is so urgent that
it could force women to grapple with the political history
around their role in the kitchen, face its complexities head
on and choose to move forward with them anyway. They
could not and did not pretend that this history did not exist.
There was an ideological issue for the women in choosing to
operate in a space that they knew was also a symbol of their
oppression and their subjugation. Perhaps they swallowed it
by never losing sight of the end goal – and we should make no
mistake, the end goal was well and truly met. In a movement
that has rightly been greatly criticised for its enforcement
of stereotypical gender roles and overlooking of women, we

must not overlook its groundbreaking impact. In fact, the programme lives on today as a government initiative, brought into place by the United States Department of Agriculture in the mid-seventies. This makes me sit up a little taller and pay attention. The Black Panther Party is far, far more than men with fists raised. It is also more than women relegated to the kitchen. Food is more than food. Women were there. Women are here. They are driving us forward. *We* are driving forward. We are driving resistance. Food is our call to arms.

WAR

With food being a weapon taken up by so many groups, it makes less sense to me than ever that the British government still seems unable to recognise that it is at war. I wonder to what extent this is because food is predominantly the weapon of the underdogs, held by the desperate, the hungry, the angry, the lost, the frozen – the sick and tired of being sick and tired. What makes this even more interesting is that, in refusing to recognise the urgency and the power of these discourses, the government also fails to recognise that the landscape has shifted. It is no longer controlling the rules of the game.

This is perfectly highlighted by footballer Marcus Rashford's groundbreaking campaign to keep British school children fed. In 2020, upon hearing that schools were going to be closing as a result of the coronavirus pandemic, his simple response was: well, what are the children going to eat? As someone who, if not for the after-school and breakfast clubs he attended, would not have eaten as a child, Rashford understood on a visceral level the vital importance of food in a way that the politicians in their gilded Westminster towers never could. Let us make no mistake: the situation surrounding food in the United Kingdom is at crisis point. According to the House of Commons Library, while there is no widely accepted definition of 'food poverty' in the United Kingdom, a household might be described as experiencing food poverty if it cannot (or is uncertain about whether it can) acquire 'an adequate quality or sufficient quantity of food in socially acceptable ways'.[12] In 2021/2 there were 4.7 million people, or 7 per cent of the UK population, in food poverty, including 12 per cent of children. In 2023, charity the Trussell Trust, which runs around two thirds of the food banks in the UK, gave out more three-day emergency food parcels than it ever had before. In 2010, 60,000 food bank packages were handed out in Britain. In 2023 it was 2.5 million. We must be very clear about this: food banks are a result of political decisions made by a government that has put individualism ahead of humanity. Austerity Britain, the years of the Tory government under David Cameron and Theresa May, and later under Boris Johnson and Rishi Sunak (Liz Truss announced austerity policies but failed to implement them in her short premiership), slashed the social safety net of the welfare system that was keeping so many alive. Combine this with the global crisis of the coronavirus pandemic and a perfect storm was created.

With this tumultuous background in place, by getting involved with charity FareShare, Rashford and his campaign gripped the nation. The government was not going to step up, that much was clear. So, much like Captain Sir Tom Moore, the elderly man who single-handedly raised billions for the National Health Service (a public-funded institution),

Marcus Rashford and FareShare took it upon themselves to ensure that schools being closed did not mean any more children would find themselves hungry. They reached a £20m fundraising target; a combined effort that swept in everyone from school children raising funds to huge corporate-level sponsorship. According to FareShare, 'Within a week of Marcus's involvement, we had half a million pounds, from people in 35 different countries. Pre-Marcus, we were delivering 930,000 meals every week. We're now consistently exceeding 2 million meals – but sadly, we're still not keeping up with demand.'[13]

A millionaire footballer taking on the plight of the children of a nation was always going to be an exceptional ground for fanning political tensions, but the government did nothing to help its own cause. What started as a simple campaign to ensure that no child should go hungry simply because schools were closing became a landmark issue of our times, in large part because of a government that failed to take food seriously – and *didn't care*.

While children were starving in their homes, food and energy bills rose faster than disposable income did. As families grappled with the dizzying rise in bills and the uprooting of the tenuous footing they had found as they got used to being locked in their houses, the government slashed universal credit payments by £20 a week – the difference between people being able to put food on the table and ... well, not. Meanwhile, according to a report from the Foreign Office, officials spent £344,803 of public money on food and alcohol in 2021.[14] Just as with Gilmore and Hamer before, the authority figures revealed themselves to be uncaring and totally out of touch. Then-Conservative MP Lee Anderson stood in the House of Commons and argued in all seriousness that food banks were 'unnecessary' because the leading cause of food poverty was a lack of cooking and budgetary skills as opposed to actual poverty. In one of then-Health Secretary Matt Hancock's early daily televised coronavirus briefings he singled out 'millionaire footballers ... to take a pay cut and play their part' – ignoring the bankers, the hedge fund managers and the government themselves.[15] Even before the pandemic, 4.2 million children were living in poverty. Footballers had not created that situation. It was a result of the decade of austerity following the government's bailout of the banks during the financial crisis. Those on benefits were pigeonholed by Tory governments as 'shirkers not workers' and were villainised by the right-wing media.[16] In fact, as Rashford knew – as so many of us know all too well – it simply is not true. The right to eat is not a privilege that we might gain access to if we work hard enough. It is a right. End of sentence.

Writing to then-Prime Minister Boris Johnson, Rashford explained:

My story to get here is all too familiar: my mum worked full-time, earning minimum wage to make sure we always had a good evening meal on the table. But it was not enough. The system was not built for families like mine to succeed, regardless of how hard my mum worked. As a family, we relied on breakfast clubs, free school meals ... food banks and soup kitchens were not alien to us; I recall very clearly our visits to Northern Moor to collect our Christmas dinners every year.[17]

Again, I come back to the link between cooking and writing, eating and reading. Is there a different story to be written here? Food banks keep so many alive, but without Rashford's campaign and the support of an entire country who knew that the way things were was simply not good enough, food banks alone would not have had enough food to meet the need. Demand is increasing exponentially, due to aforementioned policies such as the cut to Universal Credit in October 2021, the five-week wait for Universal Credit, the two-child limit, the benefit cap and the sanctions system. What's more, the statistics that we do have are just the tip of the iceberg. People typically use a food bank as a last resort – but there will be many more who simply don't even bother, especially if supply cannot meet demand. If people were solely dependent on the benevolence of food banks they quite simply would have starved. Correction: they did starve. In fact, they are still starving. The more I sit with this thought, the more noxiously egregious it becomes to me. Can we actually stop and think about the fact that in the sixth-richest economy in the world, people are *dependent on charity in order to survive – and none of us even bats an eyelid*. We have become desensitised to something that is fiercely and abhorrently abnormal. Perhaps, I think, if we cannot rely on our government, then we need to revisit this idea of the alternative family. What if food access became a communal responsibility, a shared objective? What might that mean for its future?

When you look closely, this community-led food activism has existed alongside so many major societal movements as a means of enacting radical change and, because it is ignored or co-opted or quashed by government authority figures, it often has a streak of radical protest at its heart. This can be traced from the literary salons of the 1920s where food was served alongside the exchange of cosmopolitan ideas to the very present day, with environmental activists hurling soup at the *Mona Lisa* in 2024 as part of a protest for 'healthy and sustainable food'. These protests do not centre the individual, but rather position individuals who are determined to drive change. Even at the most recent *Mona Lisa* protest, as the soup dripped down the protective glass casing, the activists removed their jackets to reveal the Riposte Alimentaire (Food Response) slogan emblazoned across their T-shirts. 'What's the most important thing?' they shouted. 'Art or the right to healthy and sustainable food?' They went on to add: 'Our farming system is sick. Our farmers are dying at work.'[18] This is just one event in a long series of food being used as a means of protest. In 2022 Letzte Generation (Last Generation) activists launched mashed potato at Claude Monet's *Les Meules* (*Haystacks*) at the Barberini gallery in Potsdam, Germany. In May 2022 a protester threw a custard pie at the *Mona Lisa*, crying out for artists and all of us to 'think of the planet'. UK climate group Just Stop Oil also used tomato soup as a weapon of choice, throwing it at Vincent van Gogh's *Sunflowers* at the National Gallery in London in 2022 before later that same day rubbing cake on a waxwork of King Charles at Madame Tussauds. In each case, food is intrinsically linked to the end goal and is being used as a way of getting people to take notice. Perhaps it is this combination of the community banding together to protest that will bring about actual radical change. Just Stop Oil spoke about their use of soup and explained that it drew attention to the cost-of-living crisis; soup is a food typically found at food banks, which are multiplying across the country. This is a powerful symbol when considered in the context of their catchphrase that people are being forced to make a choice between heating and eating. There aren't many thoughts more sobering than the fact that, while staring it in the face, some people can't even afford to heat that soup. In this context, food as a weapon of protest is complex and multifaceted: a symbol of inequality, tied up with gender, class, race, the climate crisis and the many crises that society has faced and will go on to face.

I trawl back again through the history books, wondering if this is a historical pattern that repeats, but hoping, as ever, to go back in order to move beyond. I find examples of food being right at the heart of some of the most pronounced periods of social unrest learnt, dating back hundreds of years. In England in 1776 food riots took place over the rising cost of wheat and grain. Then, there was the Irish Potato Famine (or the Great Hunger), where around 1 million people died from starvation and related causes, with similar numbers displaced and forced to leave their homes as refugees. Despite the famine ravaging the country and people starving to death, Ireland (a colony of Great Britain until the Irish War of Independence ended in 1921) continued to export large quantities of food to Great Britain. Because most of the land was owned by the English and Anglo-Irish families, it was Irish Catholics in an overwhelming majority who were forced to pay rent to the landowners and work as tenant farmers. In short, as the emerging pattern suggests, the poor – and less politically powerful – were hit hardest. Now, again, in 2024, we find ourselves in a cost-of-living crisis, defined by Crisis UK as 'a period of time during which the cost of everyday essentials like food and bills increases more quickly than average household income'.[19]

The sad truth is that, on average, poorer households spend more of their income on these essentials. Based on November 2023 Office for National Statistics data, the Resolution Foundation estimates that the inflation rate for the poorest 10 per cent of households is 12.5 per cent, whereas for the richest 10 per cent it is 9.6 per cent.[20] Making this inequality even more stark, richer households that see big increases in the cost of the goods and services they buy may be able to adapt more easily, for example by simply reducing how much they save each month or changing spending on non-essentials. In contrast, the Joseph Rowntree Foundation reported that 75 per cent of the bottom fifth of low-income households in the UK (4.3 million) have gone without essentials.[21] Overall, the worst-affected households are those on low incomes with higher-than-average energy bills (for example if they have a large family). Again, just as in Ireland all those years ago, the poorest are hit the hardest.

What would it look like if we weren't reliant on buying the (currently unaffordable) goods that we need to survive? What if they belonged not to the multinational corporations but to us – to the communities, to the people and to the land? What if we weren't feeding an endless cycle of ownership and access based on who has the most money? Demoralised now with the country I live in, I look further afield, suddenly certain that I will not find the answers I am seeking in the United Kingdom. I land upon Dr Vandana Shiva, a world-renowned environmental thinker, activist, feminist, philosopher of science, writer and science policy advocate. In 1991, Dr Shiva founded Navadanya, a national movement that works to protect both nature and people's rights to knowledge, biodiversity, water, food and, crucially, native seed. It does this by setting up community seed banks that generate livelihoods for small-scale food producers, educating them on the benefits of maintaining diverse and individualised crops rather than accepting offers from monoculture food producers. The initiative established over forty seed banks across India to provide regional opportunities for diverse agriculture. It is work that has had a real lasting impact in taking on the large-scale corporations – and winning. For example, her campaign against what she referred to as the 'biopiracy' of basmati rice by US corporation RiceTec Inc led to RiceTec losing most of its claims to the patent over the grain. In her own words:

Seed slavery is ethically important to address because it transforms the Earth family into corporate property. It is ecologically important because with seeds in the hands of five corporations, biodiversity disappears, and is replaced by monocultures of GMOs [genetically modified organisms]. It is socially important because without seed sovereignty, there is no food sovereignty. After all, seeds are the first link in the food chain.[22]

I like this idea of an Earth family. It includes us as equals with – one with – the land we live off. As ever, where money and power are involved, the notion of family, or community, floats away, as ownership, what belongs to whom, and who has the right to access what takes its place. I come back again to Rashford, recognising that perhaps the most effective way to truly challenge those in positions of power is by doing it together. Rashford was a vital figurehead but his campaign succeeded because the country got behind him. Even more than that, it was a solidarity built on those who had come before him: yet again, a going back in order to move beyond. Often in interviews, he takes the time to recognise those who have walked his path first; the ancestors who played a role in the campaign reaching the point that it did. When speaking in a BBC documentary about his mission, it was his mum that he passed the light on to, making sure that she was centre stage. He insisted that the new FareShare depot in the north-west be named in her honour not his and, when winning his Sports Personality of the Year award, posted on social media that it was his mother who was the real woman of the year. I think again of ancestors, generations of us building networks to support each other and pass hope on, a small kindling into a flame. Food can be a means of community cohesion, solidarity and integration – as I discovered during my time in Jamaica and to a certain extent when I was in Paris – and as I am discovering now by connecting women who lived hundreds of years before me with a millionaire footballer with a heart. We are building a network.

Dr Shiva's work in the space of seed sovereignty serves as a useful example for how this can exist within food ecosystems. We can help each other to create the networks that will provide us with healthy and sustainable means of survival. As pioneered by Fannie Lou Hamer, when we have the capacity to take empowered and informed action surrounding our own food stories, we all win. I decide to take this a little further, looking deeper into examples of food and seed sovereignty. La Via Campesina, an international farmers' organisation founded in 1993 in Mons, Belgium, formed by 182 organisations in 81 countries, defines food sovereignty as 'the right of peoples to healthy and culturally appropriate food produced through ecologically sound and sustainable methods, and their right to define their own food and agriculture systems'.[23] Seed sovereignty, therefore, is the right of small-scale food producers to use, save, exchange and plant seeds. Seeds have long been a symbol of solidarity, used as a symbol of growth among those who work with and live off the land. In the Catholic faith they are a symbol of hope and transformation. In Indigenous cultures like the Hopi nation, sunflower seeds symbolise bounty in their harvest festivities. Ukraine's sunflower became a global symbol of lasting peace during the Russian invasion. And in many, many rural communities, women have a particularly special relationship with seeds, recognising the importance of healthy seeds as the lifeblood and source of strength for the plants and animals that exist right at the heart of our food systems.

Women's seeds are particularly unique because they exist in a space that is solely controlled by the women farmers. While certain crops are grown by people of all genders (typically maize, grains and other staples) and may have been purchased or donated, women's seeds are the main space where a rural female farmer can harness her independence. It is up to her how many of her seeds she plants and up to her how she might fight to save them in the event of a natural disaster or drought leading to the crop's failure. It is also a space where women farmers work together, sharing, supporting and uplifting their contemporaries. In an arena where women might not possess finances in the actual physical form of money, their seeds exist as a means of financial security. They are a safety blanket – and means of survival. They also hold a vital link to those who have gone before. Collecting and preserving these seeds is a sacred act that is often passed down through the generations. It is the ultimate display of the brilliance of matrilineal connections – and sustenance of community.

While a symbol of solidarity for so many, seeds have also been a mechanism of capitalist control when they are monopolised by the huge multinationals that seek to place their stamp of ownership on everything they come into contact with. Just like children being able to have a breakfast before school in Oakland in the 1960s, and being able to have lunch in the UK in the 2020s, sovereignty is not just about having the freedom to use food products in whatever way one chooses; it is also about bonding together to ensure that access is available to all, not swallowed by the heavy jaws of corporate interest. Without this united front at a local, grassroots level and the understanding that the global food regime is destroying our precious natural resources faster than they can be regenerated, we risk forever destroying our food systems – and with them the gorgeous, glorious communities that are right at their centre. If I take all of this to its logical conclusion, seed sovereignty is necessary for food sovereignty, given that seed is the core of agricultural production – but it also means that none of these could exist without the women who, quite literally, hold them in their hands.

OUR EARTH FAMILY

Hands. What powerful, harmful, gentle, loving tools we have. We carry with us, everywhere we go, the capacity to do such good, to bring such beautiful, pure kindness. We also carry with the same ferocity devices of destruction. We have the capacity to wreak havoc with these tools of ours. I think again of my certainty that we don't need to eat – should not eat – meat. If we are already parasites, destroying the Earth, eating meat takes this to a deeper, darker level, tying murder into an already failing system and so inevitably setting us up for negative cycles doomed to pull us apart rather than bring us together. It certainly doesn't align with the idea of an Earth family, or with a globally united drive to save our natural food networks. I check in with myself. Perhaps seven-year-old me had not been a silly little child who watched a silly film and took the silly decision to stop eating animal flesh. Perhaps, the instinctual, heart-led decision from she who did not wish to have blood on her hands might teach us all something about what the future of food could look like if we dared to let it.

I start with the environment. The impact of the meat industry on our climate crisis is overwhelming. Food is responsible for a third of all greenhouse gas emissions. According to the United Nations, global farmed livestock accounts for around eleven per cent of all human-made greenhouse gas emissions.[24] Livestock farming leaves an enormous carbon footprint, contributing to the degradation of land, water, and coral reefs as well as deforestation and the devastating loss of biodiversity. When it comes to climate change, according to Julian Savulescu, the Uehiro Professor of Practical Ethics at Oxford, livestock farming contributes more greenhouse gas emissions than ships, planes, trucks, cars and all other transport put together.[25] A study from *The American Journal of Clinical Nutrition* found that a meat-eater's diet requires seventeen times more land, fourteen times more water and ten times more energy than that of a vegetarian.[26] Quite simply, we will not meet the global goals of COP* and the United Nations Sustainable Development Agenda if we do not rapidly – and significantly – cut down on our meat consumption. We have to also consider the impact on global hunger: feeding grain to livestock who will go on to be killed in order to feed humans simply drives up global demand, which in turn increases grain prices and therefore makes it even more difficult for the world's poor to afford the grain they need to eat. It is a vicious circle that makes little sense. In the same study, Professor Savulescu estimates that if all grain were fed to humans instead of animals we would be able to feed an extra *three and a half billion people*. Again, I look down at my hands, seemingly so capable of causing

---

* The Conference of the Parties, the main decision-making forum of the United Nations Framework Convention on Climate Change (UNFCCC).

death and destruction. If we strip away every single other argument, I still fail to understand how we might be okay with having blood on our hands. In what world is it possible to see that as anything other than a total failure of humanity? Many of the conditions that animals are kept in are barbaric. I imagine their short lives: caged and terrified before they end up in some plastic packaging and eventually on a plate. So what might a world without meat actually look like? Is it even possible? According to the BBC, if vegetarianism were to be adopted by everyone by 2050, seven million fewer people would die every year. If the world were to become vegan we would see eight million fewer deaths.[27] Lost biodiversity would be returned to its rightful home. Creatures like wolves, previously pushed out because they posed a threat to the cattle due to be slaughtered for meat, would return. And our bodies would benefit too, with health benefits including a reduced risk of dying from heart disease, fewer cases of type 2 diabetes and a lower risk of some cancers.

It isn't straightforward though – for as long as there are rural farmers who depend on the meat industry to survive it seems very difficult to find a way to end the global consumption and trade of meat without still causing some harm. Certain types of extremely dry farmland such as in the Sahel land strip next to the Sahara are not good for much else other than raising livestock. If we take cattle rearing out of the equation, we are removing a means of creating a sustainable livelihood from these farmers. Again, dynamics of power are essential here, as is context. Local farmers who live from the land and have always done so are not causing harm on the same level as the huge multinational corporations who seek profit above all else. I am still plagued by the question of the plight of the animals. If, in my imaginative dream-land scenario, meat-eating was banned overnight, where would all the animals go? Many of them would not be able to simply return to the wild. After generations of breeding for a specific purpose, many animals are now so far removed from their ancestors that they simply couldn't survive in their native landscape. Have we created an unsolvable problem? I come back again to the link between the land, what we eat, how we eat it and the environmental impact of all of our actions. The connection between our earth family and how we are bound to it, intrinsically connected, feels important. As I think about this more closely, I realise I need to live it for myself. I stand up. I leave my house. It is time to meet my earth family. It is time to get back to nature.

I walk, contemplating how we can protect and maintain our food networks in the communities around us without causing undue harm to our planet and its inhabitants. I will always be meat-free, I cannot see a world in which that would ever change – and I will continue to advocate for the benefits of a meat-free lifestyle, but can I do more than that? Am I, eating fruit and vegetables that have travelled thousands of miles, really any better than the local farmer providing for their family with the animals who live metres from their home? Taking in the land around me, I again challenge myself to think bigger. Certainly, I can opt for my local farm shop instead of going to the big supermarket. But can I take it further still? Can I grow what I need for myself, just like my Aunt Eseen? Can I live cleanly and simply, and share with my community? Can I help them grow? Is that how I will protect my Earth family? I walk, scanning the landscape, searching for foods that intrigue me. Foods that look good, smell good, that I simply sense will taste good. The berry we pull from a bush or the apple we take from a tree. Foraging is an act of inherent curiosity. It is an act of belief in the magic that the natural world has to offer us. It is also overlooked, more frequently, as an act that will sustain families, build communities – even heal a broken heart, restore a bruised body.

The global pandemic brought back to the mainstream quite how we might do well to continue to consider the fallacies in a food supply chain so artificial and rigid that entire lines of produce can simply dry up while, on the other hand, livestock are euthanised in their thousands. According to the European Food Information Council, roughly one third of all food produced for human consumption is wasted.[28] That's the equivalent of going into a supermarket, buying three large shopping bags of food and then immediately throwing one away. This occurs across the entire food supply chain and, if food waste were a country, it would be the third largest source of greenhouse gas emissions (after China and the US).[29] Food is wasted for many reasons, including not looking 'perfect', being close to an arbitrary 'best-before date' and simply not being used, for reasons that I imagine are something similar to, as my mother would say: 'people's eyes are bigger than their bellies'. Post-pandemic, as we gave those statistics more thought, many, for the first time, asked themselves the question: where is our food coming from? The further I trace the lineage of women, of networks and our relationship to food, the more I realise that the act of foraging was a deeply essential practice to their survival. For us today it continues to exist as an example of something we can hold up when seeking out ways to bed roots and grow. Foraging practices are not new. We have been deep in nature searching for our next meal for millennia. Some of these practices still exist en masse among certain tribes. There are the Khoisan, San, and other African-Indigenous tribes – the oldest in South Africa. There are the Hadza, a hunter-gatherer people who live in Northern Tanzania. They are generally considered to be one of the last remaining hunter-gatherer tribes on the African continent, with just 1,300 members left. They do not have domesticated livestock, something which makes my heart lift, ever so slightly. It may not be an example of what a meatless society might look like, but it is an example of how to live off the land – and with minimal waste and destruction. The Hadza prove that this is possible, surviving by foraging for edible plants. Theirs is a nomadic, clutter-free existence and they live in temporary shelters made of dried grass and branches, their very few possessions making it easy to pick up and move on. It is a start.

The more I research, the more I see again the power of connections, of generations passing on knowledge and of our own accountability to our ancestors to keep these traditions and these recipes or ways of being alive. Communities have been living off the land for centuries, long before it became economically and politically interesting to the powers that be. Historically, especially in the US before the end of slavery, knowledge was passed in hushed whispers between Black and Indigenous people. It was solidarity but it was also survival. In order to make proper meals out of the scraps they were given they needed to become well versed in the natural means of sourcing food: foraging, fishing, gathering. When slavery was abolished, officials moved quickly to make it impossible for individuals to benefit from land that they didn't own. And, unsurprisingly, the recently emancipated people were not likely to own land. Within a couple of generations that knowledge had all but disappeared. So, for Black and Indigenous people to forage today is actually a deeply political statement.

Connecting the ways of our ancestors with a twenty-first-century consumer is not necessarily the most straightforward process. Most of us probably don't really want to live off the land. Who isn't partial to a Deliveroo after a long day? Alexis Nikole Nelson, more widely known as social media star the 'Black Forager', is one of the individuals who is making it her life mission to change this. She describes foraging as:

> ... a very fun way to say, I eat plants that do not belong to me and I teach other people how to do the same thing ... It's like Disney World, but full of plants and much cheaper food. You walk in and you see this very vibrant ecosystem that we are a part of. And there's something so fulfilling about it, right? You're just like, I pulled this out of the ground, and now it's sustaining me! So I look into natural spaces and I just see wonder.[30]

Foraging, for Nelson, feels as though she has a blank canvas in front of her; a field of fresh snow just waiting to be rolled in, she is first to arrive at her very own Disney World. Her sense of 'wonder' at the open space in front of her is certainly infectious, but I do wonder how relatable it is. She talks about an ecosystem that we are all a part of but I can't shake the feeling that it might somehow be something of an exclusive club.

Presumably encountering this response all too frequently, Nelson spoke to *Ebony* magazine about why it is important for Black people to educate themselves more on foraging, referring to the historical connection that we have to it as a people. Again, I am struck by what we owe to our ancestors – the path that they have already laid for us if we just look closely enough:

> There is a rich history of Black foraging in [the United States], but due to Jim Crow era laws driving generations of Black folks away from the 'great outdoors' for their own safety, we're disconnected from that past. We're so disconnected that some folks don't think it's 'for us', but it is.[31]

We were forced inside to 'protect ourselves', and yet, actually, I think this has made us more at risk. I think of my love for the water – the grieving, healing and becoming that has happened to me on my early morning swims in icy cold lakes, rivers and tidal pools. I then think of the sorrow that always envelops me when I consider that my mother, along with so many Black people, cannot swim – will not swim. Is there an inherent trauma in the water itself? Did we shy away from it because of the boats, ready to take us, ready to destroy us? We must reclaim these spaces. They are ours. I know that this is happening in the swimming community. I am one of the voices speaking out. I feel a thrill as I see Nelson lay out in no uncertain terms that foraging is also for us. We belong in these spaces. But still, my south-east London neighbourhood is more concrete than jungle. It doesn't feel as straightforward as simply stepping out and collecting berries from bushes or a mango from the tree like I did with my Aunt Eseen. Where and how can we live from the land in the environment around us? Just like with anything, a proper education is essential. As much as we look at nature with wonder, we should also respect it. Learning how to be in and around nature is not impossible. It is something that is very much available to us, and individuals like Nelson are playing a vital role putting the spotlight on this proper education.

Through speaking about the potential that the land holds for all who step out of their comfort zone to meet it, Nelson is making foraging accessible for all of us – bringing it to our doorsteps. I begin to learn from her too and feel myself swell with wonder as she opens my eyes to the possibilities of what is existing right around me. My world expands, my very own adventure playground shining with luminous ideas. Blackberry bushes, oak trees, even dandelions. All of these exist in urban environments and, according to Nelson, we often miss them simply because most of us don't pay attention or don't know where to look. The birds and squirrels get to enjoy them instead. I want us to join them.

We can start by simply taking a walk. Get out into your neighbourhood or community and just take a look. Breathe in its scent. Get familiar with its terrain. Understand its landscape, its DNA. And, as you breathe out, open your eyes. What plants do you see? What do the trees look like? Are there seeds or berries growing here, scattered there? It might even be useful to take a notebook or make notes on your phone just so you have the option of looking things up later if need be, or noting patterns. As with everything, exercise caution. Don't just put something straight in your mouth. Work to identify it. Garden centres, gardeners, nurseries, the internet – we have a wealth of information available to us. Nelson also helpfully notes that it is useful to wear comfortable but protective clothing to avoid getting scratched or stung, and to bring some other practical items such as a small pair of scissors to cut trimmings and possibly a pair of gloves for anything that might be prickly. It all feels so doable. I feel capable of doing it, and this excites me. We don't need any special equipment or upbringing. All we need to do is be interested and curious enough to try. Foraging is for all of us.

I am drawn to this idea of seeing wonder in spaces that we should always have had the right to access – spaces that were taken from us when they should never have been closed to anyone. In her groundbreaking work *Black Food Geographies: Race, Resilience and Food Access in Washington D.C.*, Dr Ashante Reese lays out the importance of finding a way to sustain ourselves and creating practices that mean we can make spaces our own. She says being able to rely on oneself is a survival mechanism. It is a means of creating communities that can exist outside of philanthropy or government aid, something that we know to be more important than ever as food banks fail to meet the growing need and authority figures turn a blind eye. In this sense, foraging becomes a safety blanket and means of knowing we can be responsible for our own health, our own survival and, crucially, the growth of our beautiful Earth family. Pulling on my gloves, I smile to myself, humming as I think *foraging is a way of knowing that every little thing is gonna be all right.*

PART III

GROWTH

Dessert
noun

The sweet, usually last course of
a meal.

Where we breathe, we reflect and we heal.

HOMEGOING: OR, WE GO BACK SO WE CAN MOVE BEYOND

I come from Northampton in the East Midlands, a place where what is left of the high street alternates betting shops with Wetherspoons pubs and off licences with names like Krates and Amazing Savingz. Growing up, getting out into nature and being outside – with the land – became something of a solace. Cycling, running and walking anywhere I possibly could became both a physical respite, a means of escaping the confines of my physical reality, and also a mental hideaway. When my thoughts overwhelmed me, or when I needed a way of coming back to myself again after being away or experiencing a seismic 'life shift', I was able to reset myself in nature. There is certainly a peace, a sense of healing that comes from simply existing in the place we came from and the place we will all return. Ashes / dust / and all of that. So I keep walking. I keep cooking. I am sure that the answer is close to me; at my feet or on the tip of my tongue if I just hold out long enough. As I walk and as I eat it occurs to me that an appreciation of nature and an appreciation of food go hand in hand. It is a care for something that is a part of us but also exists beyond us.

Nature clears my head. Sometimes I find my words there. And sometimes, I embrace the sanctity of silence. I find that I can form my thoughts in a way that they feel as though they came from the landscape. Robert Macfarlane, the nature writer, also writes about this relationship between language and landscape. Upon realising that the *Oxford Junior Dictionary* had removed words such as 'adder, ash, beech [and] bluebell', deeming them no longer relevant, and replaced them with 'attachment, broadband, celebrity and chatroom', Macfarlane set out to find living, breathing examples of places where words float into the lexicon of local communities like clouds melting away to become part of the sky.[1] I learn about dialect from my own Northamptonshire hometown: the thawing of an icicle is to 'ungive' and 'crizzle' describes the freezing of water, evoking the sound of a natural activity too slow for human hearing to detect. Such words are transporting. Just as scent is so evocative of a time – a place – a person – so too do these words take me right to the places they are bringing to life.

I am struck by the thought that if language can bring us closer to nature it can also, surely, bring us closer to ourselves. Language, via the land, can reconnect us with the human condition; what it means to exist. Just as introducing veganism worldwide would enable lost species to be returned to their homes, so is this restoration of language also a means of bringing lost ways of thinking back to us. What Macfarlane is essentially doing is working to bring literacy and the land back together. It is a restoration of sorts – a 'rewilding' of lexicon that, if you dig deeper, reveals who has had access to the land and, more crucially, who has had it taken from them.

Rewilding, in our practical understanding, is seen as a large-scale conservation effort with the goal of restoring sustainable biodiversity and ecosystem health by protecting core wild areas, providing connectivity between such areas and protecting or reintroducing apex predators. It isn't lost on me that all of these efforts are simply attempts to mitigate the harm wrought by us as humans in the first place. They are only necessary because the balance of the ecosystem has been disturbed – and we were the ones who disturbed it.

Is there something inherently complex about the coloniser working to 'rewild' and undo the damage that they inflicted in the first place? The damages wrought on our natural world came, more frequently, from empires that were referred to as 'civilised' in an attempt to make 'civil' those that they now wish to 'rewild'. There is an innate and unfathomable paradox there. I can't quite make sense of it. I wonder, again, if the answer might be found in nature, in food, on the land. Is it possible to be a part of this world, to exist in line with its plate tectonics, breathing its beauty, walking to its beat – without needing to destroy it? Where do we sit, we who have been of the land, in the land but not historically permitted to own it, victims of a most violent theft? The more I try to understand it the harder it becomes to process. The colonisers came and took. Now, of course, they have come to love the land just as those who were there first did and many of them want to fight to protect it. Ostensibly, this shouldn't matter, but in reality it comes back again to the language. *We had the words before they even spoke.*

Vertamae Smart-Grosvenor speaks beautifully to this, bringing us back again to the power of language as a tool of the revolution. While I am searching for answers to this seemingly impossible question of whether anyone can really possess the right to claim ownership over any types of food or land or natural order, I stumble across her recipe for 'so-called okra', pertinently titled 'Name Calling'. She states:

> If you are wondering how come I say so-called okra it is because the African name of okra is gombo. Just like so-called Negroes. We are Africans. Negroes only started when they got here. I am a black woman. I am tired of people calling me out of my name. Okra must be sick of that mess too. So from now on call it like it is. Okra will be referred to in this book as gombo. Corn will be called maize and Negroes will be referred to as black people.[2]

She isn't saying that Black people are the only people with the right to any one type of food, but what she is doing, very clearly and pointedly, is reorienting us. *We have been here*, she is saying. We may have been written out of existence but that is on them. In my recipes, in my network, in my cultural and social exchange of food – in my kitchen – they are on my terms, and they will never call me out of them.

GREENS

Green
Leafy
Purple sometimes too
Bruised
Beaten
But back again
Rising
Always rising
Cared for
Nurtured
Like the collards
Like the kale.

Kale is now the buzzword of every health-conscious individual. Not wanting to simply accept this without knowing why, I do my research. It turns out that kale is an exceptional source of vitamin C and, importantly for a vegetarian like me, also of iron. The vitamin C supports growth and immunity and helps repair wounds. Iron is one of the body's most needed minerals, contributing to red cell production and oxygen transportation as well as reducing fatigue. According to the BBC, kale contains four times more vitamin C and twice as much selenium as spinach, as well as other nutrients such as vitamin E, an antioxidant. It also contains many of the minerals that our modern diets lack, providing plant-based calcium for strong bones and teeth as well as low levels of oxalate, which makes the calcium absorb more easily. Couple this with the potassium it contains and kale also helps to maintain a healthy blood pressure as well as manage cholesterol levels. The same BBC article also suggests that kale is rich in cancer-protective substances such as sulforaphane and indole-3-carbonol as well as phytonutrients lutein and zeaxanthin, which support eye health. In short, I reluctantly agree, it is one of those foods that is truly deserving of its 'super' adjective.

Its origins are in the Middle Ages but I think we tend to think of it now as something newer, more recently 'discovered', and this affronts me, just like I am affronted any time someone suggests in all seriousness that America was 'discovered' by Columbus only a few centuries ago. We don't have to look too far back into kale's history to see its roots in its close relation – collard greens. Collards were one of the few vegetables that African Americans were permitted to grow for themselves while they were enslaved and so over time they became a staple food. Because of this, for years, collard greens were looked down upon – dismissed as a food belonging to those who legally did not even possess the right to their own surname, much less the right to be a pioneer in shaping the cultural narrative around food. It is perhaps unsurprising then to note the discomfort around the rapid rise of collard greens in the mainstream landscape as a buzzy 'health food'. Many who remember a very different story feel their own sense of affront at this. In 2016, a Whole Foods store sparked mass outrage by posting a recipe on social media that suggested collard greens should be cooked with peanuts. While ostensibly the indignation was centred around the idea of putting nuts in collard greens, it ran much deeper too. It was also about the upmarket and, let's face it, mostly white clientele-based Whole Foods trying to impart knowledge to Black people about something that they had been doing for centuries. CNN's Cara Reedy wrote of the event: 'I was annoyed too, because like other African Americans, I'm tired of people "discovering" things that have been a part of Black culture for hundreds of years ... What African Americans reacted to ... is the way their culture has been co-opted.'[3]

Language is just like peanuts in collard greens. It will inevitably morph and transmute, coming and going, rising and fading along with the warmth of the sun's morning kiss and its goodnight embrace each day. I don't actually think we have lost our language. I think our words are here, they were always here and they still exist. We just need to search for them, and it might mean traipsing the land, calling out into the red dust and the vast fields for something – for hope – for deliverance. But we will find it. I know it. Just like so-called okra we will not be called out of our names. In fact, the more I think about it the surer I become that there is a beauty to be found not only in reclaiming our missing words, but in crafting and cultivating a new language too; writing ourselves into spaces that were denied to us. This might mean looking for ways to meaningfully and sustainably connect with the land that do not ignore the differences in our language, but it will also mean embracing the notion of change – and cycles of the Earth. Facing the sun. The coloniser and capitalist culture that sits at the heart of environmental destruction with its foundations in white supremacy, we see you. But you shall not win. This is our kitchen now.

THE LAST SUPPER

GARLIC STOCK CUBE PASTA

Put a pan of salted water on to boil and add in the pasta.

Chop an onion and as many cloves of garlic as you like (I use at least five).

Gently fry the onion and garlic until soft. While they are cooking, take a small cup of olive oil and add a vegetable stock cube. Using a fork, break down the stock cube so that it blends with the olive oil.

Mix pasta, oil and garlic and onions with a healthy dash of black pepper.

This one is really personal. It first became part of my life aged eighteen in the cheap vodka-induced haze of the slopes of Val d'Isère. I was on my first ever ski trip in the Christmas holidays during my first year of university. I had saved up every single penny from the supermarket job I worked on Wednesday nights, Thursday nights and Saturday mornings, scanning food I couldn't afford as I thought about the essays I needed to write, the night out I would race back to make, the hangover I was trying to suppress. Cavolo nero; Greek yoghurt; organic New Zealand lamb; Merlot; oyster mushrooms; orecchiette – I stuck a sticker over the clock on my till so I couldn't count the time, couldn't wish my shift away. I made a lot of daal that term. Lentils were cheap and the daal was filling and delicious. By the time I got to the Val d'Isère mountains, I felt a curious sense of freedom. Even the word skiing felt curiously exotic in my mouth. I would taste it, savouring its texture just as I would stick my tongue out to taste the snow, delighting in its icy thrill. I ate ice obsessively at that point, seeking to fill something.

Laura was the mother of our group. She was a fearless free spirit with a mass of beautiful curls and dark-ringed eyes. She loved to cook. I was mesmerised by that about her. The ski days were long and physically exhausting. We worked hard and I worked harder, desperate to keep up with my new friends who had skied since they were babies; a gaggle of ducklings being led to the pond. If the days were long the nights were longer. Snowy hikes down or up to the bar or club of choice that evening. 'Minesweeping' drinks because all of our money had been spent on getting out there. We had nothing else for spending. It was vital that we prepared. The dinner before the night became a sacred routine. We would stumble in from the slopes, eyes shining, faces glowing as we stomped the snow off our boots, shook off our coats. We would change, shower and perhaps have a little nap. Then began my favourite part of the evening. We prepared to eat each night as if it was going to be the last. It was always simple – and as affordable as we could make it. Pasta, vegetables and – Laura's speciality – the addition of the garlic and vegetable stock cube. It was delicious. It was salty, filling and sustaining; it replenished us after the day's physical activities while being a sensible choice for the night ahead.

I never expected that I would take Laura's garlic stock cube pasta forward into adult life – it felt very much of a particular place and time – but I couldn't get enough of it even after Val d'Isère, and it became my go-to dish. I taught it to my friends, made it for everyone I knew. Just as I had when Laura made it for me, people appreciated its simplicity and its flavour. I make it now when I'm feeling like I could do with a comforting pick-me-up or when I am craving something slightly salty. The process of finely chopping the garlic, or crushing the stock into tiny pieces – melding it with olive oil – is familiar to me, as familiar as the memory of me, Laura, Holly and Claire sitting around that table after a day of feeling the sun on our face and wind in our hair as we flew down the slopes; the world at our feet.

The following year, I came crashing down. I had fallen for someone – fallen in the full-blooded, you-are-my-everything way that eighteen-year-olds do. For reasons I will never understand and in ways that I see no real use in reliving, he broke me. And once again, as my little world started to unravel, my appetite was the first thing to go. It happened almost instantly, and I remember the peculiarity of once again finding that feeling of *not wanting to eat*. Eleven-year-old me had come calling. Sixteen-year-old me was saying hello. Hello, old friend. I felt sick, as though food would only compound my pain. Something felt too high up in my chest.

I can barely swallow my own saliva. How could I swallow food?
Maybe this is heartbreak. Maybe this is grief.

Maybe it is part of their plan to reduce us, to undermine us as much as they possibly can, so that even our place of sustenance, happiness, hope and joy – *the thing that keeps us alive* – is no longer ours.

It was different to what had happened when I was eleven and sixteen, when stopping eating was an active choice. I couldn't eat, even though I desperately wanted to. The joy of the flavours – the sensations – the *experience* of eating was gone; my life felt muted with the loss of it. Colours weren't as bright. Sounds were dimmed. The world felt too loud and too quiet all at once. I retreated into myself, screaming silently. I was hungry but I couldn't eat. Did this mean I wouldn't make it to the morning?

I once read somewhere that for some people anxiety is like a hidden spice in food dishes. I understand that. I wanted to eat because I wanted to be whole again. I wanted to heal. I wanted to sustain myself until the dark waters had subsided. But I couldn't and so I seasoned every attempted meal with my anxiety and silently starved; far, far away from the girl who grew up with the land.

Healing comes in many forms, different for all of us – but once again I found myself, almost a year later, seeking solace in nature. It is as though the more that I discovered of the world and of its cold, clinical cruelty, the more I wanted to retreat into the rolling landscapes of hills and the soft crash of waves, filled with the promise of washing me clean, starting things anew. I needed to start again. The me who had existed up until that point was gone. Lost to the muted inadequacy of a stolen appetite and an innocence forever taken. I thought bitterly of the perfectionist student, top grades, loyal friend, joyful; unfailingly joyful. The girl who ran marathons, jumped into lakes and skied down mountains an hour after putting skis on for the first time in her life. That girl was gone. I didn't even know who she was any more. Temporarily, I hoped somewhere deep inside me, but temporarily means nothing when you are drowning. I still couldn't find her.

Knowing only that I needed to get far away, I landed on the idea of Madagascar. It felt about as far as I could imagine, both in terms of geography and also of physical distance from the life that was causing me such pain. After meticulous research I decided that I would stay on Nosy Be, an island off the north-west coast of mainland Madagascar. It had volcanic lakes, over one hundred species of lemur, intricate and undisturbed coral reefs – and, most importantly to me at that time, almost no other humans. I would spend my days teaching a handful of children in a tiny village and I would live simply, from the land. Eating meant being a part of the full cycle of sourcing fresh ingredients and preparing them myself, cooking them over a campfire. It sounded perfect. I settled into camp life, enjoying the simplicity of its routine and the meditative, peaceful effect it had on me. There were about eight of us in total staying there and everyone except me lived off fish, freshly pulled from the Indian Ocean. As the only vegetarian, finding meals that didn't contain meat became my sole responsibility. I took personal pleasure in the challenge of scanning the landscape for succulent fruits or finding ways to be creative with rice and beans, delighting in the surprise of my campmates as I introduced them to other ways of eating. I lost myself in it, but in a good way this time. I became a part of the landscape.

I like the idea of foraging for food, foraging to be all right, foraging to simply be. And in the process of being – of carefully collecting, cultivating and preparing – I somehow feel again this pull to my ancestors, an unshakeable sense that we are looking back in order to move beyond. It is our small act of being accountable and of being a part of what has gone before. It is our way of saying, 'Hey, we aren't going to forget about you. We are keeping your legacy alive.' And in the process, of saying to ourselves: you're going to be okay. Foraging, crafting quietly revolutionary worlds between the lines of recipe books – even simply sharing mounds of pasta with friends – however we look at it, holding ourselves accountable to our ancestors and keeping the legacy alive is a way of taking care not just of ourselves but of each other too. It shows food as an art, cooking as a ritual. It shows us that food is a place of sanctuary where nothing can harm us. It's gonna be all right.

I often feel like this when I swim too. There is such solitude in the water, but it is also a space of deep connection. To see waves meet horizon and know that I am a part of that – I am a creature of the sea – fills me with a sense of belonging that I never knew was available to me. It is often a place where I feel most connected to those I have lost. There is an otherworldly sense to the water; a reminder that we are all from this Earth, of this Earth – and it is back to the earth that we will return. This became my daily routine that summer in Madagascar. I floated with the waves. I began to heal.

KEEP ON KEEPING ON

Food and food customs also sit hand in hand with the practice of creativity, a means of writing new worlds out of tired and disappointing ones. Out of nothing – or 'the profound desolation of [our] reality'[4] as Toni Morrison put it – we can often find new possibilities for creation. Breaking point can also be making point. Hope often resides in the darkest of situations. When the unimaginable happens, from somewhere deep within, people still manage to wake up each morning, put one foot in front of the other and sometimes even to rally. Perhaps the fear of what might happen is worse than the reality of actually experiencing it. Perhaps, once the worst happens, fear loses its sting. After all, some of the most beautiful things can be born from tragedy. In the heart of conflicts, we can still see acts of kindness if we look for them – mass rallies for ceasefires, prayers for a brighter day. Out of the dark expanse of the plantation fields rose spiritual songs. Families of daughters killed by their partners or sons killed by the brutality of state forces found charities in their names, vowing to ensure that it never happens again. One person's loss becomes their mission to save someone else from the same fate. Darkness does not equal hopelessness. Pessimism, it occurs to me, alongside apathy, sometimes comes from those who have never really had to know what it is to go without or to lose. Is it easier to find hope when you have had it snatched from you? Or, perhaps, is it a case of survival?

Smart-Grosvenor puts it perfectly:

> The slaves were just adapting to a language that wasn't their own. They were from many tribes, and plus the masters didn't talk too tough themselves. So they took the English language and did what they could with it and it was beautiful. Black people are the only people in this country who speak English and make it sound musical.[5]

When thinking about this need – compulsion – to survive against all odds, food starts to sing. It is our lifeblood. It is what we are made of. I once heard someone say that the reason Black people are so good at looking towards the future is because the past has been so hard to endure. In a history with so much trauma, why would we ever choose to look back? But the creativity, resilience and hope that is crafted into the very mechanisms of our ancestry has taught me so much. I dare to dream differently. I dare to wonder what would happen if we – as a people – dared to look back in order to learn how to survive. What if we dared to look between the cracks of the images of raised fists, bowed heads, swollen bodies, sexualised caricatures and instead pulled joy from those crevices, tasted laughter in the missing history and found magic in the in-between? In the context of food, what if we dared to look back as we continue to seek out the gaps; the ingredients

missing from our pages? What might we find there? Food as
a necessity, yes. But also, food as happiness. Food as an art
form. Food as escape, as healing from pain. Food as what we
put into our bodies, and what we take from the world – as life.

I think back to my time in Nigeria, back to my being
muted. During this same trip, I learnt to cook jollof rice. I
also learnt about the complex, bloody history of rice, from
Gullah Geechee red rice to Charleston red rice. I can't stop
thinking of the red. Is it anger? Is it blood? South Carolina's
wealth was made from rice grown by enslaved Black people,
brought over especially for their skill sets in cultivating the
grain and setting up irrigation systems. Shipped to the States
precisely because of this desired skill, they then grew, har-
vested and milled what went on to become part of a hugely
profitable global economy. The red was virulent then, raging.
But I don't want the red to stay angry. I don't want it to tear
me apart. I don't want to look back any longer. Instead, I look
for examples, ways to make the red become passion or fire or
even a slowly growing warmth. As so often happens, I find
solace in the words of Vertamae Smart-Grosvenor. She has
a recipe for Red Rice that speaks directly to me. It speaks
directly to an order of resilience and survival: 'Fry smoke
bacon in skillet and then add your fresh tomatoes. Cook for
a hot minute. Add cold cooked rice and cook for another
20 minutes.' She then moves seamlessly with no apparent
explanation for the transition (her mind working in a way
that I recognise so intuitively, neural pathways firing at all
angles) into describing how she 'really loved Aunt Rose'. This
progresses into a description of the state of the living quarters
that Aunt Rose inhabited: 'a furnished room in Harlem on

131st Street' – 'a dump' that she paid $100 a month for the privilege of living in.[6]

Smart-Grosvenor goes on to describe how cooking good meals in such conditions 'would be way beyond the capacity of most women'. 'Most women', although not explicitly stated, seems to mean 'white women', for it is this thought that leads Smart-Grosvenor to consider how remarkable it is that 'Black people in spite of all the misery and oppression . . . keep on keeping on'. She almost seems to inspire herself with this thought, and in her trademark style she begins directly comparing white people and Black people, demonstrating what she sees as the resilience demonstrated by Black people that is not demonstrated by their white counterparts. She depicts their survival of the Middle Passage as 'a credit to our race', talking about the lower suicide rates of Black people with an overall message that 'white folks just seem not to be able to take it when times are hard'. She is typically tongue in cheek in tone, stating that 'if they [white people] had known about neck bones and dry peas they might have realised that they could survive'.[7]

From both my own life experiences and active work in suicide prevention, I know that it is not the case that Black people are somehow immune to the all-consuming thoughts of suicide ideation that curl around your throat until they have squeezed your last breath from your lungs. I know for example that, in the US, according to the Centers for Disease Control and Prevention (CDC), young Black people have the fastest growing suicide rate compared to their peers of other racial and ethnic groups. I know that in many global majority communities, the mechanisms to speak out about mental health – and to be listened to and taken seriously – are not a given. It is very hard to address an illness if we do not have the language to even acknowledge its existence. I think again of survival: what it means, why some 'survive' and others don't. I think of my own loved ones, who could not to bear to stay on this Earth a moment longer. I mourn.

Back in my kitchen, I prepare one of my most loved – and most simple – dishes.

KALE SALAD

Juice of a whole lemon
Small cup of olive oil
Garlic
Salt
Pepper
Pecorino cheese, finely grated

Pour lemon juice into a small cup of olive oil, using two parts olive oil for every part of lemon juice.

Crush a couple of garlic cloves and stir into the cup.

Wash the kale leaves before massaging them and chopping them finely. It may sound strange but, whatever you do, don't forget to massage it. It helps our bodies with digesting the leaves – and is also strangely therapeutic.

Drizzle the olive oil, lemon and garlic over the leaves. This will make it zingy, zesty, delicious and flavoursome. Add a pinch of salt and freshly ground coarse black pepper and a sprinkle of pecorino.

Just as kale is about health, it is also about survival. We have to massage it before we prepare it, much in the same way that multiple studies have found that meat that is humanely killed will also taste better. High cortisol levels (caused by stress) can deplete muscle glycogen, which makes the meat tougher and in turn gives it an unpleasant taste. A recent study from the Goetheanum Section of Agriculture found that animals slaughtered on a farm had twenty times less cortisol in their blood than animals slaughtered in an abattoir.[8] Circumstances matter. Humanity matters. Our words matter. If we are accountable to our ancestors in the kitchen then surely we are also accountable to their roots – to where they have come from. More than just what has been documented in the written form and passed down in tattered notes and oral titbits, the land is tied to us. But crucially, we are responsible for moving forward. We carry the roadmap for survival in our own hands. Our feet trace the imprint of our ancestors' in the soil as we tread their path to see how the planting and growth that they did before us – for us – ensured that we weren't left hungry today. It still nourishes and sustains us. It lights our way. It helps us grow.

As I mull this over, I walk and I cook, as though the answers will find me in the wind or at the bottom of my saucepan. It is tiring, but in that delicious achy way that physical exertion wraps itself around your body – almost like an embrace – as opposed to the chokehold of being mentally drained.

I think again of the relationship between language, loss and food. Why, when my heart breaks, do I lose my appetite? I open the news and words dart out at me, piercing me with their unforgiving tip. Genocide. Rape. We will stop the boats.

Anyway, living under this cruel unsmiling canopy of deepest grey endless drizzle unforgiving heavens is a lifestyle choice. You want it. I stop eating. Of course I stop. I cannot have while so many have nothing. And sometimes I think I have no words, too. But then I march I speak I s c r e a m. And someone says: thank you. Now I will too. And someone else says thank you. You saw me. And sometimes I say thank you. I can speak now. So even when I think I have lost my voice it is there, somewhere. But what about eating? I mean, of course, we eat to survive – it's all the more reason to do so when so many cannot. But when that happens, I don't think it is a joy any more. It becomes a compulsion, of sorts, a need to fill a hole that actually I don't think can be filled.

If you really think about it, it is unsurprising that food is connected in such a base and real way to matters of the heart. When our heart breaks it breaks deep inside us. When we read the news of another of our sisters missing or an entire people being massacred, we feel it low in our bellies, right in the place where we expect to fill ourselves up and replenish ourselves for a day ahead. How do we connect on a real level? How do we actually open up, how do we actually listen, how do we actually feel – not just for ourselves, but for our earth family too?

In the words of Audre Lorde, 'there is no such thing as a single-issue struggle because we do not live single-issue lives'.[9] Our lives are messy and overlapping, a smörgåsbord of struggles, of resistance – and of overcoming – all feeding the other. Our experiences are entangled. One ends as another begins. We cannot separate and neatly categorise the brilliant, devastating, complex minutiae that make us who we are. Nor should we. More than that, though. Lorde's words are an unmistakable challenge to each one of us to unite. If we help each other in our individual struggles, then the collective liberation from these darker times will be all the sweeter when we reach the other side. In other words, let us sit down at the table – together – and let us eat.

I come back again to the many, many times throughout my life where I have lost my appetite and quite simply stopped eating. I think of what I know to be true for so many of my friends, my loved ones and even strangers I have never met for whom the scales start to tip, their bodies become their prisons and eating becomes a slow form of torture. The complicated thing about food is that for everything else that it is – all of the creativity, the joy, the unusual and the daring – it is also a necessity. Childishly, I find this unfair. A painter will not be hospitalised if they decide they do not want to paint. Similarly, an avid moviegoer who stops watching films is not cause for immediate concern. But to stop eating is to reject – somewhere, somehow – a desire to live. Food is life. To eat is to live. Is it as simple an equation as that?

I let this percolate. One thought will not leave my head. I want to eat. I want to live. Despite both of these facts, I have grappled with the 'loss' of my appetite since I was eleven years old and I still do not really possess the language to articulate why. I don't know where to turn with the conundrum. The days of nineties diet culture are long gone, but disordered eating remains a cultural phenomenon, it's just less overtly discussed now. We talk about health, wellness and fitness, but behind our empty words we are shrinking; without the vocabulary to delve into what, why, or how. I don't want to make myself smaller. I want to be seen.

Lorde also wrote:

When you are hungry
learn to eat
whatever sustains you
until morning[10]

For the first time, I find myself moving away from Vertamae Smart-Grosvenor and her theories of how to survive. Maybe it isn't about survival at all, but instead, the simple act of sustaining. Not forever. That might be beyond our reach. But if we can just keep on keeping on until dawn breaks – well, maybe that in itself is our radical act.

I take up my own challenge on a trip to New York (not that I require much persuasion). I am an ever-fierce defender of my independence and the beauty of travelling – eating – forging a life alone. Today though, sitting on a sidewalk in New York's Lower East Side one sunny October lunchtime, I am struck by the way that so much of how I operate when I am alone is geared towards food and thinking about where my next meal is coming from. It isn't even an interesting thought, but I feel an urgent compulsion to say it to someone. It occurs to me – a little jolt in my stomach – that I don't want to be eating alone any more. I no longer relish its magnificence. The more I travel alone and eat out alone, the more I am beginning to wish I could share. And then, almost as if the food gods themselves were listening, three elderly Canadian sisters sit down at the table next to me. This is New York after all, so our knees are practically touching – and they are typically friendly. They seem dismayed to see me travelling alone and invite me to join them. I tell them that I too am one of three sisters. I hope we will be like them when we are their age. They laugh, delighted, and welcome me over. I am one of them now. It is the happiest I have been all day.

Later that week I have lunch at a gorgeous Italian place in Greenwich Village on my way home one rainy afternoon and I feel bereft. It is a sorrow for the conversations I am not going to have. Food is joy. Solo eating is radical joy. But food is also communal. It is community. I am missing my commune.

The sun will rise. We must rise to greet it – even if we don't want to see it – even if we don't want to eat. We must encourage others to do the same. I'm not sure that 'survival' can always be the end goal. It feels mammoth, requiring a conviction that we might not always have inside of us. For the first time, I realise, that is okay. Sometimes it is enough to simply make it to the faintly optimistic pink of a new day. No matter how bad things get, down on our knees, hanging on by a thread – each meal that we prepare and share is our radical act. It is our very own rebel take, our tiny subversive declaration of hope as we cry out that *we want to see morning.*

WHEN QUEENIE CAME TO TEA

YORKSHIRE PUDDINGS

Sunflower oil
Plain flour
Eggs
Milk
Salt and pepper

Drizzle oil into your muffin tin and place in the oven to heat up.

Beat flour and eggs to make batter.

Little by little add in your milk and keep whisking until there are no lumps.

Season with a touch of salt and pepper.

Evenly pour into the muffin tin then cook for around 20 minutes until they are puffed up and golden brown.

Make sure your guests are seated and ready a few minutes before your puddings come out of the oven. Yorkshire puddings are light, they are delicate, and they lose heat fast. Like time and tide, a Yorkshire pudding waits for no one, so you had better be ready.

'Here you go, love. A Yorkshire tradition. Enjoy,' says Kathleen, proudly hosting her future daughter-in-law for the first time.

Queenie sits back, hesitant, six eyes watching her expectantly. Future mother-in-law, father-in-law and husband. Family special. Mustn't let them down.

And yet. Confusion clouds her gratitude. She cannot help but look to her future husband, eyes wide with empty-stomached curiosity as she looks down at her plate of Yorkshire puddings and back to the expectant faces. Kathleen stands, going to collect something from the kitchen. Queenie takes her chance, turns to her future husband and under her breath, as quietly as she can, asks: 'Is this all we're having?'

Future husband laughs at the innocence with which the question is asked. It is an innocence that masks hunger; and masks a shock that a plate of food could have no meat, no vegetables, no spice, no flavour.

'My love,' says future husband with a smile, 'here we have Yorkshire puddings as our starter. It's a Yorkshire tradition.'

Queenie laughs, delighting in her own mistake. Kathleen returns, smiling at beautiful young Queenie, who smiles back. She sits. They eat. Jamaica to Yorkshire. Food is food. Love is love. Life is sweet.

I used to sit in raptures when my dad recounted that story of the first time my mother met his parents. My eyes would glisten with delight at the thought that she couldn't possibly have known that more food was on its way, more food was to come. Food is personal. It is of us. It encompasses our likes, our dislikes, our personalities. Different moods inspire different tastes and we eat accordingly. Do we want something salty (to cure the hangover) or light (to sustain us but not swamp us) on a summer's day? Do we want something sweet because life feels sharper than we can bear? Do we need to take a break, because food itself has become the pain source?

Food is community. It is sharing. Sometimes your parents can't say, 'I love you' but they can ship you off to university with a week's supply of home-cooked food. In the case of my parents, food was the meeting of two different cultures, bonded by love. It is meant to be shared.

I caught a plane recently. A four-hour flight to just north of the coast of Morocco. A Moroccan woman sat next to me and we briefly bonded over our curls. It was a beautiful, innocent encounter. About thirty minutes into the flight she got out a salad she had prepared and nudged it in my direction: 'In my culture we cannot eat without first offering to whoever we are with,' she told me. I was touched but explained that I was fine. She insisted – and so we flagged down a member of the cabin crew, who gave us a spare fork. I ordered some olives, which I in turn shared with her, and together we connected over the simplicity of a makeshift meal. We found ourselves talking about bigger things; her opening up about her sorrow that her children have gone off to university now and me about my sense of rootlessness – my need to find where I belong. She opened her iPad and began to show me her favourite meals. There were photos of ones that she had made and screenshots from various online sources. She talked me through each one in detail and my heart swelled with her warmth, the obvious passion and the storytelling; the language that she had for each one. There were the meals that she cooked for her children, how she was adapting those recipes now that only she and her husband were left at home. I saw how broken she was by this and thought again of my own mother. I haven't considered enough how all three of her daughters leaving home might have broken her too. I also see how, when we are all back together again, her language of love is baked into the dishes she prepares for us – our favourite food items that she buys and packs the fridge with. The childhood favourites that we haven't eaten for a decade now, except for when we return home. Back on the plane, the conversation turned to artichokes as my new friend taught me her favourite way to prepare them – how to break the leaves down to get to the heart, and what can be achieved with the simplicity of a dressing of olive oil, lemon and salt. And, as we connected over food, podcasts and our favourite places to visit, I started to feel, so fully, the power of the community. It turned out we didn't live too far from each other back home in London. We exchanged numbers and planned to go for a walk together.

There is so much to unlearn. How can we teach ourselves that our bodies are beautiful? How can we teach ourselves to find the joy in food again? How can we connect with a stranger on a plane and begin to repair something inside us that was broken? I turn back to the land. Surely, if I move through it – move back to move beyond – I will once again find the answers from my ancestors who knew something about what it meant to survive.

Again, as is so often the case, I find answers with the recipes of Vertamae Smart-Grosvenor. She is a consummate storyteller and seeing the way that she simmers and reconfigures a dish we think we know to serve up an entirely different outcome makes me think what might happen if I used food as a means of writing myself out of situations that were not of my choosing. It also makes me want to look for other women throughout history who had done so. Instead of writing for us a tragic tale of the lot of her Aunt Rose, Grosvenor both illustrates her resilience and reverses the power dynamic. Aunt Rose is shown to be the survivor, making something positive out of the situation that, according to Grosvenor, 'most women' would be incapable of rising out of. It's electrifying. I feel myself rising with her.

I keep rising as I continue to assert my existence in food spaces, filled with confidence from my interaction on the plane. I plant seeds. I tend to a young apple tree, not knowing if I will be in the same place long enough to see it bear fruit but doing it anyway. I swim, letting the icy water course through my entire bloodstream. I am alive, even when I don't much want to see myself in a swimming costume. Doesn't matter. I am moving beyond. I drink in my discoveries about other women from the recipe books of our history, feasting on their contributions before allowing them to marinate in my mind. Honouring. Paying tribute. But then, a new feeling. I want to know how we fit into their story. What spice or flavour or secret ingredient can we bring to their menu? How can we make it sweeter, or more nutritious? What can we bring to the table?

Once again, I am struck by the importance of looking back and piecing together as a means of taking us forward. Life is not a series of random events, and neither is our food history – or indeed our eating habits. At a recent Food Studies conference I attended at Leeds University, scholar and culinary anthropologist Psyche Williams Forson stated somewhat poignantly that: 'We have to remember that food is part of a compilation of objects. Food is not just food.' It is comprised of connections: to history, to culture, and to us – the future. People's experiences of food are inevitably tied up with their upbringing, their background, their lifestyle and even their individual perspective. There are those who eat for pure sustenance and those who eat for the delight and delicacy of flavours. Food can also exist as a symbol of what divides us in society. For example, in a culture that opposes food waste, many react with disdain to groups such as Just Stop Oil using food as their weapons. Sociologist Pierre Bourdieu suggests that food can define the very limits of group boundaries. He distinguishes between 'the taste of necessity', which is essentially foods that are filling and affordable – more typically associated with the working classes – and 'the taste of liberty or luxury' for those who have the luxury of not only needing to eat to live but being able to enjoy the experience of eating. We have the capacity to break this down if we choose to.

I circle back again in my mind to the question of whether Black people starve themselves if the very language and the mechanisms for recognising that starvation do not exist. I ask myself who has the right to talk about what and create recipes from what and whether it is possible to claim ownership over anything that is from the land – of the earth – that existed before us and will remain long after we have gone. I don't have the answers to this. I don't know. You cannot take something from a group of people who have nothing. If you try to do so, you will lose. You will start with something and gain nothing. You can't drag someone down who is already at rock bottom. You don't know what they are growing beneath them. You don't know how tall they will be when they rise.

We can eat to live, to give our bodies the energy they need, but we can also engage in food practices as a most heartfelt protest. We can savour the succulence of a berry, the rich heartiness of a soup, the sensory decadence of an exquisite piece of chocolate. The delicate process of consuming our entrée, indulging in the flavours and the experience of it, is part of the path we pave for our future. Each individual aspect in a meal is essential in creating a complete whole; each 'course' is informed by its predecessor. I think this is what I mean when I say that food can teach us to look back – to look behind – but not to get stuck there. We do not have to shy away from the past, but nor are we beholden to it. Entire families are fed with a little bit of nothing, seasoned with love. We are accountable to our ancestors, but we are also accountable to ourselves.

PART IV

SURVIVAL

Digestif
noun

A beverage consumed after the meal to
help digest the food.

Where we digest, we process and we look for the moon.

THE MOON

Defiant, filled with all that I have consumed, I gaze up – and out. There is a Japanese poem that I love:

> Barn's burnt down
> Now I can see the moon.[1]

When the unimaginable happens and we are brought to our knees, there is nowhere we can look except up. We cannot give up. We must keep looking for the moon. Up, up, up.

Where food is concerned, the more I look for it the more I see examples of building towards the moon. When you are on the ground with nothing, you can build anything you want. My work as a gender expert relies specifically on analysing situations with the objective of understanding how certain contexts might have different (read: better) outcomes if they employed a consideration of gender roles and dynamics. It occurs to me – and I am quickly proven right – that this is especially true in contexts of food (and specifically food security). According to the United Nations Food and Agriculture Organization (FAO), women make up nearly half of the agricultural workforce in developing countries. Despite this, they far too frequently have less access to resources and opportunities concerning agriculture and rural livelihoods than men. A different FAO report states that if women farmers had the same access to resources as male farmers, they could bring 100–150 million people out of hunger.[2] That figure takes my breath away. Women hold at their fingertips the power to give unprecedented numbers of people one of their most basic human rights – the right to eat. Poverty is more than a humanitarian issue. It is also a question of gender – and of equality. Actively fighting to create opportunities to uplift women through food opens doors for entire communities to improve their nutrition security as well as their social and economic well-being. It allows for all of us to see the moon.

I read an interview recently in which Dr Maureen Miruka, Director for Gender, Youth & Livelihoods for CARE International, highlighted the fact that, despite women being farmers, innovators and decision makers, 'they still face social norms and barriers that prohibit them from fully expressing their leadership' in these fields.[3] Even with all the evidence pointing to the contrary, women as primary farmers and producers in such a large part of the world continue to go unrecognised. It feels like a hopeless situation. But then, as I begin to search, I discover that there are countless examples of trail-blazing women who are changing the narrative around food security and working to end global hunger, just as the women of the Black Panther party worked to get hungry school children fed all those years earlier. I become hungry myself, tracing the stories of leaders such as Mariana Estrada

Avila and Teresa Lamas from Rome, Italy, who founded the Global Campaign for the Empowerment of Indigenous Women for Zero Hunger, a campaign that seeks to create awareness around Indigenous women's roles in the food system. The simple fact of recognising that hunger and malnutrition will not be eradicated without the empowerment of Indigenous women is quietly radical. I reflect on how we can and should all seek ways to bring greater awareness to the essential role played by Indigenous women, returning to the question of foraging these fields and finding ancient languages that we must respect and preserve in the landscape.

Next, I lean into the work of activist Kafi Dixon from Massachusetts in the United States. Dixon founded The Common Good Project, the first farming cooperative in the city. Its goal of creating opportunities for economic development out of access to fresh and – most importantly – local health foods is empowering women and in turn fostering a thriving community. This speaks directly to the work of New Yorker Tanya Fields who founded The Black Feminist Project, an 'organisation that looks at the intersection of food and reproductive, class, gender and racial justice to empower Black women.'[4] The project has its own farmland, beautifully named Black Joy Farm, where they host workshops and curate accessible programmes led by women of all ages to bring about lasting social change.

One of the biggest problems thus far has been the relative dearth of literature on what precisely these kinds of organisations that are empowering women through food can do. Pioneers such as Dr Wanjiru Kamau-Rutenberg from Nairobi, Kenya are facing this head on, highlighting the importance of research in changing the narrative. Kamau-Rutenberg is the executive director of African Women in Agriculture Research and Development (AWARD), a 'career-development program for women agriculture scientists in sub-Saharan Africa. AWARD provides fellowships focused on teaching research and leadership to foster the success and security of African smallholder farmers. It is also working to transform the growing awareness of gender issues surrounding agriculture into policies and programs.'[5] A fellow Kenyan, nutritionist Maureen Muketha, founded Tule Vyema, an organisation with an educational goal at its heart: teaching women how to use sack farming, completely removing the need to rely on expensive equipment and so creating a sense of economic liberation. Tule Vyema also undertakes awareness-raising educational schemes around nutritional health for young unemployed women, again bridging the gap and empowering those who stand to gain most – and teaching them to bring others up with them.

Muketha is not the only individual who has been cultivating practices to connect with the land. Farmer and educator Leah Penniman co-founded Soul Fire Farm in New York in 2010, with the mission to end racism in the food system and reclaim the ancestral connection to land that her people possess. Soul Fire Farm's mission is to train Black and brown people in farming, subsidise farm food distribution and work to help their people find agency within an unjust food system. Working from the basis that the food system as it currently exists was built on exploitation and that generational wealth needs to be rebuilt, returning the land to where it came from, there is something pleasingly simple about Soul Fire Farm's aim. Just as with Hamer before her, Penniman and her colleagues from the Soul Fire Farm approach the land always from the perspective of communal work, using Indigenous farming techniques and honouring those practices that have gone before but also working to provide ingredients for those who they are supporting to feed themselves. In doing this they are also providing the way for communities to learn to cultivate their own food. Food education is vital – and transformative – and the dating back of these practices to the ancestors helps us to keep their names on our lips.

I come back again to Rashford and to our communities, our networks. By looking out for and building *with* each other, we all create space for more brilliance to come through. There are many things we can all do to make this happen and they all hark back to us daring to dream bigger, to see bigger, to be bigger. How do we begin?

Well, we need to collect more data that is separated by gender to better understand women's role in agriculture and be able to quantify their work. That is the only way to divert more financial resources – which in turn becomes practical results. We need to develop best practices that relate specifically to gender. We also need to think about schedules and timings so that women (who especially in these contexts are more likely to have caring responsibilities) can participate in training and other activities. We need to direct awareness campaigns towards people of all genders, breaking down stigma and spreading the word about the infinite possibilities of land ownership and working with the land. I come back again full circle to Georgia Gilmore and her mission. There is something so profoundly moving about the simple act of her taking one of the very few gifts that society deemed acceptable for her to have (and even then, with conditions placed upon it) and using it to uplift an entire community. I am struck again by the quietly radical hope that food offers. Not everyone can be a Fannie Lou Hamer, or an Alexis Nicole Nelson, or a Marcus Rashford. It isn't about that. It is about showing up wherever – however – we can. It is about knowing what our gifts are and what we can bring, not questioning and second guessing and trying to make it something that it will never be. It is also about recognising the unique power of cooking – a power that even front-line activism does not possess. Cooking restores – keeps alive – those in the present moment but, at the same time, it builds a foundation for those who will come after. It is an urgent, present mechanism of survival while also building the foundations of a radical and beautiful future.

OUR MOTHERS

We don't cook because of our mothers. We didn't – despite what society would have us believe – learn at their feet. Hair in ringlets, Bessie Smith playing in the background. We cook because we want to. Because we can. Because cooking for us equals triumph – freedom – moving through. It is an opportunity for us to reclaim spaces that we were written out of, but also for us to acknowledge those of us for whom cooking was not a freedom, but rather an imposition. The act of cooking itself is now something that we can take forward precisely because our mothers couldn't. Yes, we are standing on the shoulders of giants, but we are standing with integrity and honour. We are standing on shoulders that exude lyrical liveliness and creative cuisine. They are shoulders that quashed the notion that they could ever be relegated to a box or single story. That isn't enough though. There is still more. In cooking our own way out of trauma or foraging for freedom, or finding order in the disorder of an illness that for so many doesn't even exist, *we are those giants*. We are cooking, crafting and creating new narratives; a language that is entirely our own. It is with this great responsibility that we are carrying on our backs and with our chest that we will tear down those stories that imprison us. They will not triumph. They will never win.

I feel buoyant at the thought that if we choose to keep thinking in this way – to dare to dream differently – we can find deep within ourselves the energy needed to go forth and continue the work that our ancestors have begun. We can cook them back into existence, together, forming an ecosystem built upon kindness, solidarity and sustainability. Hands outstretched, connected as we breathe life into each other and, somewhere along the way, into ourselves. Food is communal. We are a community. Actually, our mothers' kitchens are our own. And maybe they were all along. Let's cook.

EPILOGUE

MUSHROOMS

I watch an interview with climate activist Mikaela Loach in which she compares the drive to bring about social change with the underground mycelial networks of mushrooms. As she explains it, there are millions of fungi living under the ground. These fungi connect with each other and other living beings. As these beings are formed, and grow, and die, they talk to each other, building networks of communication between much of what is living in the ground and passing the nutrients on to keep these living things alive.[1] I am surprised to learn that these mycelia are in fact the largest organisms in the world. For me, what makes them so incredibly powerful – and inspirational to us in our own journeys to see things differently, and keep going – is that these networks exist underneath our feet right now, *even though we don't see them.*

All we end up seeing are the few mushrooms that have emerged through the ground; mushrooms that we might dismiss as irrelevant or even harmful. I catch my breath as I watch Loach speak, my understanding of the role that every single one of us can play forming in my mind, and then out of it – soaring with the possibilities of what we might do, the changes that we might make. I take heart. I take *great* heart. Often in our work, with our drive for tangible results, we only think about the mushrooms emerging above ground and forget about the underlying mycelial networks keeping the whole system alive. We think about the big picture: ending poverty, ending hunger, achieving gender equality, becoming antiracist. But what this can also mean, when we don't see immediate results, is that we feel dejected. We think we have failed. *This is not true.* If we can dare to dream bigger – to see things differently – and to think about radical social change in the context of the mycelial ecosystem, then we can take new strength as we bound forward, secure in the understanding that none of the mushrooms or the trees or the entire system would even exist if it had not been for the network of brilliant, persistent, rebellious individuals who just kept going – even, in some cases, without ever being recognised. We cannot give up on our hope of a brighter future. Our work, even if we don't see it today, is fuelling the mycelial networks that are growing the mushrooms that will sustain us tomorrow. We are stronger together. The mycelium knows that. Georgia Gilmore knew that, as did Marcus Rashford, Fannie Lou Hamer and my thoughtful, diligent Aunt Eseen. We are united in our mission and if we can just keep striving to continue being accountable to our ancestors, to recognise the inherent value of food as an overlooked and powerful means of resistance, as a driver of social change, a crafter of identity and means of writing our own stories, then the possibilities feel endless. We don't need to change the world overnight. We just need to keep reaching out to those around us, trusting that if we do so, the mushrooms will come. Barn burns down? So what. We know how to survive. We can break bread with our neighbour. We can help them rebuild the roof. All we need to do is just keep nurturing our mycelium ecosystem. Then we will see the moon.

> when life gave us lemons
> we planted our feet
> rooted ourselves
> and expanded

NOTES

PART I

1. Smart-Grosvenor, Vertamae, *Vibration Cooking: Or, the Travel Notes of a Geechee Girl* (New York: Doubleday, 1970)

PART II

1. Fisher, Abby, *What Mrs. Fisher Knows About Old Southern Cooking, Soups, Pickles, Preserves, Etc.* (San Francisco: Women's Cooperative Print, 1881)
2. Demuth, Jerry, 'Fannie Lou Hamer: "Tired of being sick and tired"', *Nation* (1 June 1964) <https://www.thenation.com/article/archive/fannie-lou-hamer-tired-being-sick-and-tired>
3. Ibid.
4. Ibid.
5. Ibid.
6. Ruiz, Michelle, 'How Stacey Abrams is turning the tide in Georgia', *Vogue* (5 November 2020) <https://www.vogue.com/article/stacey-abrams-georgia-vote-turning-the-tide>
7. Washington University in St Louis, 'Interview with

Georgia Gilmore', filmed interview, <http://repository.wustl.edu/concern/videos/8049g7144>

8. Gebreyesus, Ruth, 'One of the baddest things we did: Black Panthers' free breakfasts, 50 years on', *Guardian* (18 October 2019) <https://www.theguardian.com/us-news/2019/oct/17/black-panther-party-oakland-free-breakfast-50th-anniversary>

9. Blakemore, Erin, 'How the Black Panthers' breakfast program both inspired and threatened the government', History.com (6 February 2018) <https://www.history.com/news/free-school-breakfast-black-panther-party>

10. Milkman, Arielle, 'The radical origins of free breakfast for children', *Eater* (16 February 2016) <https://www.eater.com/2016/2/16/11002842/free-breakfast-schools-black-panthers>

11. Ibid.

12. O'Connell, Rebecca et al., *Living Hand to Mouth: Children and Food in Low-income Families*, Child Poverty Action Group (27 August 2019) <https://cpag.org.uk/policy-and-campaigns/report/living-hand-mouth>

13. Adams, Tim, 'Marcus Rashford: The making of a food superhero', *Guardian* (17 January 2021) <https://www.theguardian.com/football/2021/jan/17/marcus-rashford- the-making-of-a-food-superhero-childhunger-free-school-meals>

14. Dreyer, Pete, 'Tory government spent nearly £345,000 of taxpayer money on food and alcohol, according to Labour', Squaremeal (16 February 2003) <https://www.squaremeal.co.uk/restaurants/news/tory-government-taxpayers-restaurant-spend_10393>

15. 'Coronavirus: Premier League players should take a pay cut – Matt Hancock', BBC (2 April 2020) <https://www.bbc.com/sport/football/52142267>

16. Adams, Tim, 'Marcus Rashford: The making of a food superhero', *Guardian* (17 January 2021) <https://www.theguardian.com/football/2021/jan/17/marcus-rashford- the-making-of-a-food-superhero-childhunger-free-school-meals>

17. Ibid.

18. Slow, Oliver, '*Mona Lisa*: Protesters throw soup at da Vinci painting' (28 January 2024) <https://www.bbc.com/news/world-europe-68121654>

19. 'The cost of living crisis', Crisis <https://www.crisis.org.uk/ending-homelessness/the-cost-of-living-crisis/>

20. Brewer, Mike et al., *The Living Standards Outlook 2023*, Resolution Foundation (January 2023) <https://www.resolutionfoundation.org/app/uploads/2023/01/Living-Standards-Outlook-2023.pdf>

21. 'Cost of living', Joseph Rowntree Foundation <https://www.jrf.org.uk/cost-of-living>

22. Confino, Jo, 'Vandana Shiva: Corporate monopoly of seeds must end', *Guardian* (8 October 2012) <https://www.theguardian.com/sustainable-business/vandana-shiva-corporate-monopoly-seeds>

23. 'Food Sovereignty, a manifesto for the future of our planet', La Via Campesina (13 October 2021) <https://viacampesina.org/en/food-sovereignty-a-manifesto-for-the-future-of-our-planet-la-via-campesina>

24. 'Livestock emission data at a glance', Food and Agriculture Organization of the United Nations <https://foodandagricultureorganization.shinyapps.io/GLEAMV3_Public>

25. Pickles, Matt, 'The ethical arguments against eating meat', Oxford News Blog (28 April 2017) <https://www.ox.ac.uk/news/arts-blog/ethical-arguments-against-eating-meat>

26. Pimental, David and Pimental, Marcia, 'Sustainability of meat-based and plant-based diets and the environment',

The American Journal of Clinical Nutrition, 78:3 (2003), pp. 6605–35

27. Smith Galer, Sophia, 'The consequences if the world decided to go meat-free', BBC (12 June 2017) <https://www.bbc.com/future/article/20170612-the-consequences-if-the-world-decided-to-go-meat-free>

28. 'Reducing food loss and food waste', European Council <https://www.consilium.europa.eu/en/policies/food-losses-waste>

29. 'Data point: The dirty truth about wasted food', Economist Impact (17 November 2021) <https://impact.economist.com/sustainability/ecosystems-resources/data-point-the-dirty-truth-about-wasted-food>

30. Mohtasham, Diba and Zomorodi, Manoush, 'Meet Alexis Nikole Nelson, the wildly popular "Black forager"', NPR (9 September 2021) <https://www.npr.org/sections/codeswitch/2021/09/09/173838801/meet-alexis-nikole-nelson-the-wildly-popular-black-forager>

31. Taylor, DeAnna, 'Meet the woman behind the viral account schooling us on foraging', *Ebony* (16 February 2023) <https://www.ebony.com/black-forager-interview>

PART III

1. Macfarlane, Robert, *Landmarks* (New York: Penguin Books, 2016)

2. Smart-Grosvenor, Vertamae, *Vibration Cooking: Or, the Travel Notes of a Geechee Girl* (New York: Doubleday, 1970)

3. Friedersdorf, Conor, 'What's leafy, green, and eaten by Blacks and whites?', *Atlantic* (22 January 2016) <https://www.theatlantic.com/politics/archive/2016/01/whats-leafy-and-green-and-eaten-by-blacks-and-whites/424554>

4. Morrison, Toni, 'What the Black woman thinks about women's lib', *New York Times* (22 August 1971) <https://www.nytimes.com/1971/08/22/archives/what-the-black-woman-thinks-about-womens-lib-the-black-woman-and.html>

5. Smart-Grosvenor, Vertamae, *Vibration Cooking: Or, the Travel Notes of a Geechee Girl* (New York: Doubleday, 1970)

6. Ibid.

7. Ibid.

8. Sprügel, Lea and Peschke, Jasmin, 'On-farm slaughter: Animals' stress hormones reduced by a factor of twenty', Goetheanum Section for Agriculture (7 June 2023) <https://www.sektion-landwirtschaft.org/en/sv/on-farm-slaughter-animals-stress-hormones-reduced-by-a-factor-of-twenty>

9. Lorde, Audre, 'Learning from the '60s', address at Harvard University (February 1982)

10. Lorde, Audre, 'For Each of You', in *The Collected Poems of Audre Lorde* (New York: W. W. Norton & Company, 1997)

PART IV

1. Mizuta Masahide, Japanese proverb

2. 'When you think farmer – think female!', Food and Agriculture Organization of the United Nations (17 March 2021) <https://www.fao.org/climate-change/news/news-detail/When-you-think-farmer-think-female!/en>

3. '25 empowering women reshaping the food system', CGIAR (8 March 2021) <https://gender.cgiar.org/news/25-inspiring-women-reshaping-food-system>

4. DeMarco, Carlet, '27 inspiring women reshaping the food

system', FoodTank (March 2021) <https://foodtank.com/news/2021/03/women-led-organizations>

5. 'Home page', AWARD: African Women in Agricultural Research and Development <https://awardfellowships.org>

EPILOGUE

1. @mikaelaloach and @feminist, Instagram (1 January 2024) <https://www.instagram.com/mikaelaloach/reel/C1jTilSuGZk>

ACKNOWLEDGEMENTS

Thank you to Sharmaine, Hannah, Adriano, Eleanor and the ever-dazzling team at Dialogue. Thanks to my brilliant agents Gordon and Meredith. I cannot believe I have written my second book and it is thanks to each one of you.

To my beautiful family: my mum and dad Ivet and Adrian, my sisters Laura and Hannah, my cousin Lauren, my aunties and my grandmother. Thank you to Angus and Jude and to my ever-loving friends. Grateful to all of you for making me laugh, holding me up and feeding me (in approximately equal measure).

To mes amis Parisiens and the many, many people I have shared a plate or glass with as I have made my way around the world.

And finally, thank you to the generations of women before me who taught me to cook by vibrations – and always with feeling.

Bon appétit.

Bringing a book from manuscript to what you are reading is a team effort.

Dialogue Books would like to thank everyone who helped to publish *Rebel Takes: On the Future of Food* in the UK.

Editorial
Hannah Chukwu
Adriano Noble
Eleanor Gaffney

Contracts
Anniina Vuori
Amy Patrick

Sales
Caitriona Row
Dominic Smith
Frances Doyle
Ginny Mašinović
Rachael Jones
Georgina Cutler
Toluwalope Ayo-Ajala

Design
Ben Prior

Production
Narges Nojoumi

Publicity
Millie Seaward

Marketing
Emily Moran

Operations
Kellie Barnfield
Millie Gibson
Sameera Patel
Sanjeev Braich

Finance
Andrew Smith
Ellie Barry

Audio
Dominic Gribben

Copy-Editor
Alison Griffiths

Proofreader
Jacqui Lewis